Table of Contents

I dedicate this book to my parents, Bobby and Gina Pierce. From a very young age you taught me that hard work and dedication would take me far in life. You have supported me through all the ups and downs I have had. I also want to dedicate this book to my girlfriend, Jennifer Henley. You have helped me further myself in more ways than I can name, without you I would have never written this book.

Printed in the United States of America

First Printing, 2012

ISBN 978-1-105-97550-9

www.Idea2appstore.com

About The Author

Taylor Pierce has been developing apps since Apple's App Store opened to the public in 2009. In the summer of 2010, Taylor was awarded an internship with the coveted Apple Headquarters in Cupertino, California. He has developed over 60 apps, many of which have ranked consistently among Apple's top 200. Taylor has firsthand knowledge of what makes apps marketable and profitable. As the CEO and founder of the mobile development studio Idea 2 App Store, Taylor has revolutionized the app marketplace. His mobile development studio deals with a wide array of clients from individuals' app ideas to the needs of Fortune 500 companies. Because of Taylor's direct knowledge of clients' needs, the specifics of app design, and the ever-changing app market, he has designed this book as a reference tool for success in The App Store.

Few people exist who possess Taylor's level of expertise and experience with The App Store. He has built apps for nearly every category in The App Store and has accrued financial success not only for himself, but also for his clientele. In addition to app development, Taylor also offers consulting to individuals and companies who wish to maximize their apps' performance. This book was inspired by his desire to provide exceptional consultation services for his clientele. For his personal clients, he wanted to write a book a client could read to become informed of the "ins and outs" of The App Store. It has become his business practice to require each client to read the book prior to having an app developed; with this knowledge, he hoped clients would have the understanding necessary to maximize their apps' profitability. After noticing the vast improvement of his clients and their apps, Taylor decided to release the book to the public and share his secrets to success.

Appreneurs

Preface

Appreneur – An entrepreneur who specializes in mobile apps

You are interested in making an app. You have read all of the stories of successful developers and appreneurs. You are determined to get a piece of the pie. Welcome to the app era. The world of apps is the fastest growing market in the world today, and it is here to stay. The best part is you can get in on it! Now what if I told you that without the knowledge contained in this book the odds of you making a profit are slim to none? What if I also told you that you probably wouldn't break even? There is more to apps than most people think. The average person assumes that if they make an app, they will instantly become a millionaire. The truth is without the knowledge from years of successes and failures, you just won't know where to begin.

This book contains tips, tricks, secrets, and stories from the top developers, appreneurs, and companies from around the globe. We have information from single team developers all the way to the big boys in the Fortune 500 companies. After reading this book, you will have the knowledge to bring your idea to life, market it, promote it, and sell it in a way that would have otherwise been impossible. You will know exactly what to do to make sure your app is successful in the crowd of over 650,000 apps. Before now, a book that revealed the secrets of success in The App Store was nonexistent. Within this book, you have the knowledge of years of experience from the top appreneurs in the country right in the palm of your hand.

Appreneurs

Chapter 1

"Staring at the bottom and rising to the top"

The year was 2009; I was just finishing my first year at The University of Texas. I sat in my room proud of my first year. I had decided to pay for my own college education to take the burden off of my parents' shoulders. I opened my bank account and nearly had a heart attack. I had less than 100 dollars in my account and a loan of nearly $25,000 slapping me right in the face. Keep in mind this was just my first year in college. At the rate college tuition was increasing, I was sure to be six figures in debt by the time I graduated. I thought to myself "I may have bitten off a little more than I can chew."

Mentally exhausted with the financial pit I was digging, I sat down and decided to play video games with some of my friends to relieve the stress. What happened next changed my life. One of my gaming friends pitched to me the idea of how cool it would be to track your in game stats via an app. Basically, I wanted to know how good I was doing without having to log on to my computer after each game. I literally sat the controller down and opened up my laptop. I was majoring in Computer Science at the time, and I remembered seeing the news of developers creating apps and making a considerable living doing it. My friend's random comment motivated me to immerse myself into the world of development possibilities. That summer, I spent almost every waking moment learning Objective-C and the iPhone SDK. In the fall of 2009, I released my first app. It was an interactive guide for one of my favorite video games, *Halo 3*. My app was an overnight sensation. It began to receive tons of recognition in the gaming world. I was getting emails from professional players that were using my app at events. I had companies literally blowing up my email wishing to advertise on the app. Although I was ecstatic with my success, I wasted no time before moving on to my next project. I knew that I had only scratched the surface of the potential available in the app market.

By 2010, I was earning enough money from my app to cut my loan amount by half. Finally, I was able to actually enjoy my college career; I was even able to quit my Ramen Noodles college diet. I was by no means a millionaire, but I had found the app store gold mine, and I was virtually mining away!

In my next venture, I began to create different types of applications for many specialized niches. As I tracked the progress of my new apps, I noticed apps I created for hobbies that I lacked personal interest in didn't do as well as I had anticipated. It was then that I learned the most important thing about The App Store: if you are passionate about something and know a lot about it, then you can create high quality apps that users will enjoy.

By 2012, being an app store expert was my career. I was financially secure and living my dream. I opened a studio called Idea 2 App Store (*www.idea2appstore.com*) because I wanted a way for people with no development skills to be able to sell apps and make money. If someone like me could go from living in a 400 square foot apartment and driving the same truck I got when I was 16 to living in his dream home and driving his dream car, I figured anyone could. I wanted to provide them with the opportunity to make those dreams come true.

Unfortunately, my "dream" assumption was incorrect. I had forgotten how much information I had learned in those three years. I had gathered so much data from my successes and failures that my clients just didn't know. I decided to branch out and add consulting to our list of services. Before too long, many major companies and lucrative clients were asking for my advice and seeking my counsel. During a 3-4 hour consulting session, I could take a client without even a basic idea of how The App Store works and mold them into a pro. They were able to take the skills and secrets I taught them and integrate them into their apps. It made me feel good getting phone calls a few months later from them explaining how well they were doing. That feeling of helping others achieve dreams motivated me to share the information I use when consulting with clients and create what you are about to read in this book.

Some of you might be reluctant to believe that my success can be your success. You might even be thinking, "I am not a computer programmer. How can I create apps?" The answer is surprisingly simple. The advent of swift technological advancements in our society has created a surge in the number of quality developers available. No matter your location, you can find a developer or studio that fits your needs and budget.

Without a doubt, creating apps can be expensive; expect to spend between $50-$150 dollars an hour for quality app development. If hiring a developer is your only option, consider this plan: start small and expand. Most people do not understand that apps are software and quality apps will take time. There is no way of accurately predicting what your application will make prior to checking your sales once the app is live in The App Store. Some apps *blow up* immediately, generating huge profits and some apps *tank* without any profit; such is the nature of The App Store. If you keep your first app small in the terms of price and time, you will reduce your chances of losing excessive time and money. If the application begins to generate steady revenue, then you can add features and update the application. This is the ideal business model for one reason: USERS LOVE UPDATES. I cannot stress this enough. There have been apps I have made and almost gave up on; however, after an update with a few extra features, the app sprang back to life. Quality applications are never complete. If you think your application is done, then you will soon begin to see its sales drop.

So you have an idea. What's next? First and foremost, do your research. Check The App Store and see who, if anyone, has made something similar. If you find something like your idea, you need to do three things to compete: download, dissect, and do it better. Do not think just because there is an app like yours out there that your idea is a bust. Sometimes it can be the just the opposite. The first thing you need to do is download the competitor's app. Dissect the application; find out what is good and what they could have done better. Next, read each one of the application's reviews. This is a secret not many developers/appreneurs know about. You have access to crucial customer feedback. Focus on the negative reviews. Ask yourself, "Is this a valid point? Is this something I can do and maybe do better?" Lastly, and if applicable, find the app's ranking. If you can find ranking data, you can get a general idea of the amount of revenue the app is producing. Once again, this is another secret many appreneurs overlook.

Another common misconception about app creation is that you have to be a technology genius in order to create a profitable app. On the contrary, a fellow appreneur named Benny Hsu had his app 100% outsourced and still turned a profit. His app *Photo-365* is very well done. Though you don't often read about developers making money from outsourcing apps, Benny's story exemplifies how success is possible if you know the market. I asked Benny to share his experiences, so you could see that app success is not only for the computer literate. According to Benny Hsu:

A long time ago I wanted to create an iPhone app. As a user and fan of the iPhone since the first version, I had two reasons to create an iPhone app. First, I thought it would be cool to be able to say, "Here is my iPhone app." Second, I wanted to start a business on the side. I wanted to become my own boss and stop working for someone else.

My only problem was that I had no idea how to code! I thought that was the only way to create an app. One night, I was on the internet and just happened to come across a blog about creating income online. This blogger had an iPhone app company with a partner earning thousands a month. He didn't know how to code either. He outsourced all the work. At that time, I knew about outsourcing, but didn't know the possibilities. He recommended an e-book to learn about outsourcing app development. That's exactly what I needed. I bought that book and another small e-book. Developers who were able to create a business from apps, much like what you are reading now, wrote both books, all without any coding experience.

I didn't let thoughts of failure stop me. I was determined to learn all I could and do the best I could. The app was supposed to take 1.5 months, but it ended up taking about seven months. The delay didn't frustrate me. I was really pleased with the prototypes my programmers were sending to me. I didn't want to rush it to just get it out. I wanted the app to be done well.

The app was released on August 10th, 2011. At that time, I would have just been happy to make my investment back. It cost me $1,900 to develop *Photo 365*. That was a lot of money to me, but an amount I was willing to risk. Little did I know what was about to happen to my app.

Within the first seven days, I had earned my $1119.46. This completely blew my mind. This was beyond my wildest dream. It only got better. The following week I saw *Photo 365* featured on New and Noteworthy (New and Noteworthy is a featured category selected by Apple. If your app is featured in this category, you are going to see a large influx of sales). Not only did it get featured, but also it was in the second spot from the top. While I was enjoying that feeling, that following Tuesday I got an email from Apple marketing requesting art assets. I read the email so many times just to be clear what they wanted. I had a feeling what this was for but didn't get overly excited yet. There was a lot of work to do to meet their 24-hour deadline. Luckily, my brother is a *Photoshop* wizard and helped create the art assets they needed. The contact person was really helpful in answering all my questions really quickly. That next morning, I sent off the email and waited.

On the Thursday of the same week, I was working at the restaurant. During a break, I decided to check my app's progress. I knew they updated The App Store in the afternoon, but I didn't know exactly what time, so I was not expecting much of a change. I logged onto a forum and saw a private message telling me congrats. What? I quickly went to The App store and saw *Photo 365* featured as App of the Week! I jumped and screamed like I hit the lottery. My heart was racing. I went to Facebook and Twitter and shared my excitement. That whole night at work, I couldn't stand still. It was an exciting moment that I'll never forget. The sales that week were phenomenal. Every night I couldn't sleep because I couldn't wait to wake up in the morning to check sales. I felt like a kid waking up early on Christmas day. I had become App of the Week in just my third week. Even as I type this, I find it hard to believe it happened to me.

After the first 30 days, I had earned $32,865.91. Not only did I make my investment back, but also I was able to start my own app company. How quickly life can change in just 30 days.

You might be wondering how I marketed my app. You might assume that I must have spent a lot of money. I'll be honest with you, and it may surprise you. I didn't do any marketing. I didn't spend a single penny on marketing. I had some review blogs contact me that first week and ask for a promo code to do a review. I was just happy anyone wanted to review it, so I always said yes. The biggest website to do a review at the time was *Appadvice.com*. The same day I got the email from Apple marketing, I had *Photo 365* reviewed on *Gizmodo.com*. I didn't contact them at all. That was a great surprise.

I'm proof that you don't need to have a huge marketing budget to create an app that gets seen by users and Apple. If you create a well-polished app that your target customers love, they will find it, and they will tell others about it.

I would tell anyone who wants to develop an iPhone app through outsourcing that it's not as hard as you think. At the beginning, it might seem overwhelming because you're so unfamiliar with the process. But if you don't take a chance now, when will you? If I had never taken a chance and risked failure, I would have never experienced the success that came from it.

If you wish to download one of Benny's apps or check out his blog, the details are below.

Photo 365 http://photo365app.com
Gratitude 365 http://gratitude365app.com
Get Busy Living http://getbusylivingblog.com

Benny Hsu's inspirational story represents all that can go right when you make smart development choices. The next chapter outlines specifically how to effectively develop your app to maximize results.

Chapter 2

"Choosing the right development option"

- Developing Quality Apps

I contacted Benny to share his story because it is both inspirational and relevant to the content in this book. Also, I wanted to prove the power of developing or outsourcing quality apps. He found a good target market, created an app they would enjoy, managed his users, and consequently accomplished great success. To see for yourself what a professional quality outsourced app looks like, be sure and download *Photo 365*.

When it comes to app development, you have two basic options: developing that application yourself, or hiring/outsourcing the development. There are pros and cons to both options. If you are a tech savvy programmer with some experience, then learning the language and SDK is a great idea and probably will not provide you with much trouble. You will certainly have lower overhead costs resulting in a greater profit margin if you can develop the app yourself. However, the downside is that learning the SDK takes time, sometimes more than you can spare. For example, to just learn the basics of the SDK took me around 5 months even with a good background in programming. The SDK is always expanding; I have been doing this for four years and still learn new things every day. While you are learning the SDK, someone could be developing your idea! I am not saying that developing your own idea is always a race against competitors, but it is possible that while you are preparing, another developer may cross the finish line with a similar concept. Therefore I advise if you have an idea for the next big app, or an idea that is very time sensitive, by all means have a studio or developer create the app.

Having a developer create the app comes with its share of new responsibilities and potential issues also. Most importantly, have anyone you are discussing an idea with sign a NDA (non-disclosure agreement). This document will protect your idea and your intellectual property. A few months back a client came to me with an idea for an app that I thought was very unique. They came to us because we offer s unique service where we develop the app free of charge if the idea is something we really like; in turn, they receive a cut of the profits. It is a good way for people with great ideas and a low budget to have apps developed. In this particular case, we were a bit busy and were not going to be able to start on their app for at least another month. They decided they couldn't wait and went to another studio. A few months later I noticed their app was in The App Store. I emailed them my congratulations. They didn't email me back, but called me immediately. The situation they described was that they still had not developed their app idea; furthermore, the new studio had not signed a NDA. Regrettably someone was not selling their app idea, and they had no way of proving it was their idea. Unfortunately, this is just one of many times unethical business practices have taken advantage of the inexperienced

Second, choosing the right developer or development studio is crucial. This is by far the most complicated part of outsourcing the development process. Since I own a development studio, *www.idea2appstore.com*, I am familiar with the questions and answers most potential clients will require. My insight will help you choose the right developer/ studio for your needs. The first question you should ask is whether the development studio or developer is local. A local developer will allow you to have much greater control over the development process. Most studios with local clientele have a more intimate connection with clients. Frequent face-to-face meetings are ideal for development because you will be able to communicate openly with the developer as you become more comfortable, allowing you to share your vision more completely. Generally, the greater personal handling by the local studios costs more than a free-lance developer, but the results are well worth the expense. As a matter of fact, the intimacy of a local studio will allow you to see a demonstration of your app before production, meaning you will be able to correct any errors and greatly reduce the number of revisions needed in the end; a benefit that will likely save you precious time and money. Local development studios will likely charge between $75-$125 an hour for development; this also usually includes all the necessary graphics.

Another option is remote development. Basically, developers are divided into two categories: local (which I will define as your country of residence) and overseas (which I will define as Indian, Chinese, and Russian). Both types have positive and negative aspects. Generally, local development will require more financially; however, you will likely get a much better product. Overseas developers generally work inexpensively, but may deliver subpar applications. This is usually due to a few issues; the language barrier and the education and experience of the developers. I have outsourced a few apps when I have been too busy. Of the five I have outsourced, only one came back usable. Needless to say, I don't have entire apps outsourced for this reason. Although there are exceptions, historically local developers/ studios create superior apps.

At times even overseas outsourcing can be utilized without causing the final product to suffer. When my studio gets overwhelmed with client requests, I choose to outsource some of the development. My method of outsourcing allows me to meet client expectations while still delivering a quality product. If I am forced to outsource development, I make sure that it is only the backbone and basic features of the application. Since the basic features are fairly straightforward, it would be difficult for any developer to get it wrong. After the basic features are completed, my team will then develop the more advanced feature set. My experience has taught me that this plan of outsourcing the easy jobs while keeping the major features local saves the client money and ensures production of a high quality app in a timely fashion.

Much like I do at my own studio, outsourcing the beginning design and easy features is a great way to save money and time. This is generally the most mundane part of the development process and can be handled by a relative amateur. There really isn't a need to spend top dollar when having the base features implemented. For the select few with unlimited means, you could certainly keep all of the app development local. For those who need to economize, I have determined that the hybrid development plan works well. Once you have a good base app built from outsourcing, find a quality local studio or developer. This is where having someone that is experienced matters. They will be in charge of handling the more difficult features and overall UI (user interface, basically what the user sees such as: buttons, images, animations, and icons). By doing the development process in this manner, you will save a great deal of time, money, and headache.

After you have found your developer, what should you do next? First, get a sound contract written. Fortunately, you do not necessarily need an expensive lawyer to make this happen. Search the Internet; there are hundreds of template contracts you can use. Make sure the contract grants you the rights to the source code of the application. If a developer will not grant you the rights to the source code, DO NOT WORK WITH THEM! Websites such as *www.elance.com* are great for finding developers, but are plagued with the issues stated above.

Before taking your idea to the developer, design the concept on paper. When a client comes to my studio with an application idea but no paper or *Photoshop* model, I almost instantly turn the client down. If you simply take the time to design the application, you will save yourself potential expense and frustration. Remember, you know in your head what the app needs to look like and do; nevertheless, developers cannot read minds! The more prepared you are, the better chance you have of your application being a success.

- Picking the right title

When app lovers are searching for new apps to download, they first see the app's title. The App Store loads the title of the app first and then the images asynchronously (in the background). This being said, to sell, your title must be catchy and enticing. A user needs to be able to read the title and instantly think, "I have to buy this" or "Hmmm, this is interesting, better open the details up and see more".

There are two types of titles: *plain* and *description* titles. A plain title is just that: the title of the app. This is common with popular games like: *Angry Birds, Cut The Rope*, and *Tiny Wings*. There are some advantages and disadvantages to this type of descriptor:

> Pros – These short names build great brand recognition and are easy to remember.

> Cons – Without a description following the title, they will not get as many hits for different keywords. Keep in mind that words in the title count as keywords.

> For example, if your app was called *Photo Caption – Create Pictures With Captions*, you will be able to get keyword hits for each word in the title.

Description Titles, conversely, are popular with appreneurs wanting to get a few extra hits on their keywords. The searchable keywords are broken down into 3 categories:

> Publisher Name – The publisher for the app's display name, such as Rovio for *Angry Birds*. If you search Rovio, you will see *Angry Birds* right at the
>
> > top.

> Application Title – The title of your application; this can either be the plain title or the description title as stated above.

> Keywords – Keywords are hidden to the public and are submitted with the app to The App Store.

Publisher name is the strongest powered keyword and will yield the highest ranking, followed by app title, and then followed by keywords. Also built into the search algorithm is number of downloads, downloads per day, and number of ratings and reviews. No one knows for sure the exact formula for the search algorithm, but there are a few educated guesses among seasoned developers. I assign each category stated above a point value to get an idea of how my app will rank on a searched term. The more points, the higher the keyword ranking. For example:

Publisher Name 5 points

Application Title 3 points

Downloads Per Day 2 points

Total Downloads 1 point

Keywords 1 point

Number of Reviews 1 point

To show you what I mean, let's pretend we name our publishing company (or individual name) that is to be displayed in The App Store as "Great App Publisher", our app's name is *Great App – Awesome Fun App*, and our keywords are "Great", "App", "Multiplayer", "Game".

If you search "Great App" chances are we would come up at the top because we have "Great App" in the publisher name, title, and keywords. There is some speculation that if the word is in your title, then it doesn't matter if it is in the keywords. That was true until only recently. If you searched a term, for example, "Great Multiplayer" for our game and "Great" and "Multiplayer" weren't in our keywords, then our app wouldn't have shown up. For this reason, I like to include my app's title in my keywords to be safe. For the search "Great App" we would have gotten 10 points for the searched terms regardless of downloads or reviews. That is a very good result, and it would be easy to keep a high search result for that ranking. Understand that this hypothetical scenario is an ideal case and won't work most of the time. Usually publisher name is not something you can get a hit on; sadly, that's just the nature of the beast. Although you cannot control all aspects of the keyword process, there are still ways to show up very high in the search algorithm. Initially, rank is easy to escalate with new apps, but it is much harder to achieve by climbing the ladder over time. Follow these 3 steps to ensure you are ranked high when your app is released:

1. Make sure your app has a few good keywords in the title, and make sure they are used as a description to avoid rejection by Apple. Apple does technically say not to have keywords in the title, but if they are used as a description of your app, they do not care. Take for example the app name *Gun Range – Fun Exciting Super Awesome Gun Range*. They will reject this instantly because you are using keywords blatantly in the title. Now let's say we change it to *Gun Range – Virtual Shooting Range 45+ Guns*. They will likely allow this since it is a description of what your app does. This is a fantastic way to get a few extra

keyword hits.

2. Make sure you have a good set of keywords, including your app's title name. Recently Apple changed the search algorithm where you cannot search a word in the title plus a keyword and see a result. For this reason, always include your app's title as a keyword. There are rumors that this will be changed back to the old search algorithm, but be forewarned that minor things like this are changed quite often.

3. Make sure you get a lot of downloads in the first 72 hours of your app going live. I have found out that this is the crucial time for determining where you show up in the search terms ranking. The first 3 days can make or break your app. Don't worry; there is going to be a ton of information in the book about how to get the downloads you'll need.

- Choosing Quality Keywords

Once your application is in the developmental process, there is still work to be done. This is a very crucial time to do research on the most important part of the app, keywords. Keywords, as introduced earlier, are words or phrases that users will search to find your application. Regrettably, a defined set of keywords that will guarantee your app is found and downloaded does not exist. No matter how great your application is if users cannot find it, then it will not sell. One hidden gem of keyword help is a website called *www.appcod.es*. This website is incredibly useful for optimizing search terms. The most useful part is the ability to see your competitor's keywords. This is huge! Most people do not understand the power of keywords and how they are used to increase your app's visibility in The App Store. Quality keywords will put your app in front of the most users, and because of the vast numbers of apps available to consumers, you will need all of the exposure possible. There are no set keywords that produce perfect results. Each app is different and as such requires specialized keywords.

Many developers will attempt to benefit from successful apps by including app names in their keywords. This ploy's purpose is to presumably gain traffic generated from popular apps. Although on the surface this may seem like a logical plan, it is not a good idea for one reason. In general, people don't search apps by name. They will usually enter a search term such as "fun game" or "free shooting game." This is how searching works. Take a look at the pie chart below by Chomp (The App Store's search engine provider).

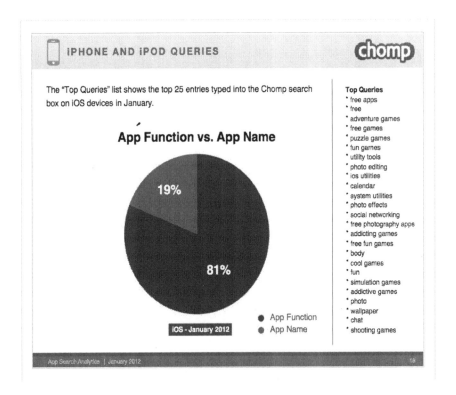

The "Top Queries" list shows the top 25 entries typed into the Chomp search box on iOS devices in January.

App Function vs. App Name

19%

81%

iOS - January 2012

● App Function
● App Name

Top Queries
* free apps
* free
* adventure games
* free games
* puzzle games
* fun games
* utility tools
* photo editing
* ios utilities
* calendar
* system utilities
* photo effects
* social networking
* free photography apps
* addicting games
* free fun games
* body
* cool games
* fun
* simulation games
* addictive games
* photo
* wallpaper
* chat
* shooting games

App Search Analytics | January 2012   18

As you can see, the majority of searches are for the app's function vs. the specific names. To the right of the graphic, a list is included of the most searched terms. If you use *www.appcod.es* correctly to track some of the top app's keywords, you will notice the same information being shown. This is something the majority of appreneurs never learn! So once you have done your research and have your keywords ready, what can you do now to ensure success?

• Designing a quality app icon

Besides the title, designing an app's icon is probably the most important factor in determining whether your app is downloaded.

Consumer research supports the fact that people like visually appealing icons. Point and case, we had an app that was really entertaining content wise, but had a really ugly icon. Sales were disappointing to say the least. In an effort to improve sales, I decided to have the icon redone from the ground up. It looked substantially better; the icon makeover gave it that visually appealing "wow" factor. Overnight, sales quadrupled and continued to rise. The app went from being ranked 157 in games to 24 in one day. Remember when I said users love updates? When updates address the issues and concerns users have, they are ecstatic to see the changes and often tell other people about the apps they enjoy.

Because visual appeal is often subjective, there is no set standard for designing an icon. Often the graphic design process is the biggest struggle for appreneurs, but there are some guidelines that can make the process less painful. First, look and see what kind of icons your competitors have. What do you like about them, or what do you dislike? Have the users said anything about the icon in the reviews? Once you have an idea for an icon, jot it down and find a quality graphic designer. DO NOT PINCH PENNIES ON A GRAPHIC DESIGNER. Graphic designers are a dime a dozen, but quality graphic designers are much more rare. Finding a designer is much like finding a developer. You need to look into their past work and see the quality in it. Remember, the icon can make or break the app. I have seen apps that had the potential to be the next viral app, but since the icon was so unappealing, users simply didn't download it. To consumers, their phone is a prized possession; no one wants ugly icons on their home screen.

When you have what you think is a good icon designed, share

it with your friends. Ask for their honest opinion. Listen very closely to any constructive criticism they may have. I would also post the icon on any forums that may be specific to your app and ask for opinions there. Two forums, _www.iphonedevssdk.com_ and _www.macrumors.com,_ are both generally good forums for this type of thing. Feedback is always important, and it is imperative to your app's success that you learn to receive it. Just because you like an icon doesn't mean everyone else will. Do not get so invested in your personal opinions and tastes that you discount valuable information. Ultimately, your goal is to make an appealing app for a user, not yourself.

- Writing an engaging app description

At this point, you developed your app, chose keywords, and designed a beautiful icon. You should be finished, right? Almost. At last, you are in the final stages of the development process. To complete the process, you need to write a great description of your app's purpose and function. Think of the app's description as a summary of what the app will do. Grab your favorite book or movie and flip it over to the back for inspiration. Imagine you are the app consumer. What could you read that would compel you to download the app? If the consumer is reading your description, they are already intrigued; either your icon or app title has piqued their interest. Now it is time to close the deal! As an attention grabber, I like to start off my descriptions with any awards or great reviews my app has received. If a popular app review website reviews one of my apps favorably, I will copy and paste the short review and site it. Users like to see this; it shows them they are downloading an excellent app. Even if you don't have a popular web review, you can also benefit from posting a specific user's review from the app's reviews section. Although anonymous reviews are not as prestigious, they are still worthwhile, especially if your app is new. After positive reviews, I then like to put the app's highest achieved ranking. Here is an example of an app review we used in our game *Draw With Me*:

> *** Top 25 Game Worldwide ***
>
> "One of the best substitutes for *Draw Something* on the market. Inexpensive, fun, and fast."

- Free App A Day

When a user opens my app, the first things they see are positive things about the app. They see it has a good ranking, and they read a positive review app in the most positive terms. Oftentimes, this positive reinforcement alone can be enough to get you that download. While you want to present your app in the most positive terms, it not advisable to invent good reviews or rankings if your app has not yet earned them. Give it some time; if after a few months you don't have a good review or high ranking, it is time to make some changes to your app because something is not right.

Once you have a good description written down, take it to an editor, or a friend that is grammatically gifted, and have them proofread it. Chances are by this point you're very excited about your app, and this can cause you to overlook a typo. Trust me, I know from personal experience how embarrassing proofing errors can be. Granted, this metadata can be changed even after an app is live, but it still makes you look bad. You want your description to be engaging, descriptive, and accurate. Despite the descriptions importance in the appeal to app users, do not be misled by appreneurs who tell you that you can get search hits for words in your description. THIS IS NOT TRUE. Your description has one main purpose: to tell the user what your app will do.

- Creating enticing screenshots

Last, but certainly not least, is the app's display screenshots. These screenshots are usually the final image a user sees before buying the app, so you need to impress them. Weary buyers are often convinced to buy an app because the screenshot sealed the deal. Screenshots are generally of two varieties in the app store: plain screenshots (which essentially are just an exact replica of the app's screens), and designed screenshots. Designed screenshots can either enhance or degrade an app depending on the quality. Most of these use an iPhone template and add cool colors and text over the plain screenshot to really make the image come to life. For ideas on how to do these well, take a look at the top 25 apps. These are usually done by companies with large budgets and have amazing graphics. But bear in mind, you can't go wrong with a simple screenshot; however, a poorly designed screenshot can have devastating results. I tested my theory a few weeks back. We had a funny picture-captioning app that was ranked number 12 in its category. The app had plain screenshots, so I decided to make some rather poorly designed screenshots and test my theory. Testing a theory on one of my top apps is not generally a good idea, but I was willing to risk it so I could have the most accurate data for my book. Almost overnight, the app's ranking fell by nearly a hundred spots. To test the positive effects of superb screenshots, I had my designer create some professional screenshots. My theory was proven to be accurate. After the new graphically pleasing screenshots, the app surged up in the rankings to number 7, even higher than its earlier ranking!

An effective strategy I like to use when making designed screenshots is to try and tell a story. If you can do this successfully, potential buyers will be attracted. Make the screenshots colorful and fun. Users are buying apps to have fun; make them entertaining! Here are the example screen shots from our photo-captioning app *Caption Me* as an example. It is very simple, but is much more entertaining than just simple screenshots.

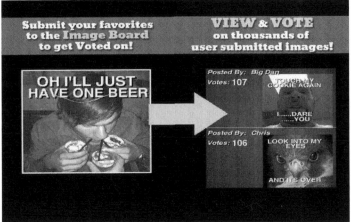

Do you see how these screenshots tell a story of what the app is and does? Well-designed screenshots like these are also more amusing and visually appealing than just ordinary, straight from the phone screen shots. If you have been researching apps, you probably noticed most of the top selling apps include well-designed screenshots. Why do you think that is? Simply put, good-looking screenshots drive downloads. The possibilities for screenshot design are endless and vary with each unique application. If you find a good designer for your screenshots, stay with them. Finding a reliable, capable designer is not an easy task, and you may have to work with a few different designers before finding one that meets your needs. My screen shots are designed by Maggie Williamson; she is very good at what she does and has a gift for being able to make the screenshots vibrant and visually pleasing. If you would like to talk to her about designing your screen shots, she can be emailed at maggieb07@yahoo.com.

Finally, you have your first app ready to be uploaded to Apple for review. Keep this in mind: Apple has become much stricter on the content they will and won't allow in The App Store. To avoid rejection, be sure to review the Apple User Interface Guidelines before submitting an app. If your app requires any type of login or sign up, provide Apple a test, or demo account, in the Review Notes section of the metadata. If you have any question as to whether or not your app may get rejected, I recommend signing up for any developer forum and posing your questions there first. My personal favorite is _www.iphonedevsdk.com_. Quality developers and appreneurs have formed a professional learning community via this site where developers will help solve your most troubling content issues. It is likely you'll see me posting on there as well. If your app gets rejected, DO NOT PANIC. I have had more apps rejected than I can count. My first reaction was usually panic over the months I had spent working in vain. Usually you will get a message from the reviewer as to why your app was rejected. Simply make any changes they ask and reupload. If you reupload a rejected app, the same reviewer will review it the second time. If it gets rejected the second time, the odds are that particular reviewer will never accept it.

To circumvent the same reviewer, change the app's title to something like a ton of random letters so you can use the app's title again when you reupload the app. Next, start the upload process again from scratch, reuploading the app. This time you will get a new reviewer, and maybe your luck will be different. At this point, you will need to create all new metadata, keywords, and screenshots. My rule of thumb is if I get rejected from 3 different reviewers, then I throw in the towel. I draw the conclusion that my app contains content that Apple will not allow. If you can find an app in The App Store that is similar to yours, but you are getting rejected just hang in there and keep uploading. It may take some time, but if the similar app was approved, so can yours. Once your app is live and in the app store, you can finally relax, right? Wrong. Relaxation of concern is the most crucial mistake amateur appreneurs make. To find out how to create considerable profits and long term revenue, continue reading Chapter 3: "Don't compete in a market, create it."

Appreneurs

Chapter 3

"Don't compete in a market, create it"

A lesson I have learned from The App Store is that apps in specialized markets can do very well. Specialty, or niche, apps are applications for very specific hobbies or types of people. The possibilities are endless: video games, sports, dogs, bird watching, fishing, astronomy, etc. Even though these hobby-targeted apps seem to only appeal to a small segment of the population, they can actually easily bring in six figures. Unfortunately, the success of niche apps is overshadowed by the more prevalent news of someone creating the next game sensation. Realistically, the odds of creating the next viral game craze are stacked against you. The stories often unpublished concern apps in specialized categories that generate tons of long term revenue and have much less competition. I reached out to a fellow appreneur, Brass Monkeigh, when writing this book. His unique series of apps not only transformed the app market, but he literally created a new genre of apps. Brass Monkeigh shares his chronicle of how business acumen can be born of personal passions and interests:

The story of Brass Monkeigh Apps begins with a familiar set of circumstances: a college dorm, too much free time, and an idea. In 2009, I was a college student taking introductory programming courses. In my spare time I, like most of my roommates and peers, spent far too many hours playing video games. Having the engineering mind that I do, I always kept a calculator next to me while I played. The purpose for this was to keep track of my kill to death ratio, which is commonly considered the primary statistic for determining the skill of a player. After every few games played, I would bust out the calculator and figure out how many more kills I needed to add to the numerator of the equation before my ratio would tick up. Streamlining this simple math equation became the springboard on which my company was launched.

Around this same time period I purchased my first iPhone. The device's ease of use and ability to support custom software amazed and intrigued me. I made it a personal goal to learn the necessary programming language and design a specialized calculator for the iPhone that would calculate and track my kill to death ratio for me, and then provide me with different statistics about it. After a month or so of saving tips from my food delivery job, I managed to scrape together $250. I then asked my parents for a loan for the remaining $200 needed to purchase a used MacBook from eBay. My first MacBook wasn't pretty, but it did the job. With only a 13-inch screen there was barely enough room to fit the iPhone simulator, but it was enough for me to design my first app.

After I had a working model of what I called the "Kill Death Ratio Improvement Tool", the question came of whether or not to publish the app to The App Store. This question did not have a straightforward answer. I had already spent $450 on this project, nearly half of which was borrowed money that I would have to pay back, and to publish my little calculator to The App Store meant signing up for the iTunes developer program, which would set me back yet another $100. "One hundred dollars buys a lot of Ramen noodles" was all I could think of. According to my logic at the time, after I convinced five or six friends to download my app, I would still be out over $90 in the long run. Thankfully, I could not have been more wrong.

January of 2010 rolled around and by that time I had repaid my parents and even had a little extra holiday money burning a hole in my pocket. I decided to sign up for the developer program and publish my app. By the end of the month, the "Kill Death Ratio Improvement Tool" by Brass Monkeigh Apps had been published to the iTunes App Store. The next day would change my life forever. After my first day, I had three sales. I couldn't believe that three totally random people paid to download the app I made. The next day three turned into five. Before long I was making nearly ten dollars a day, which meant that I would be able to recover the cost of the developer program in only a number of days, compared to the year I thought it would take.

The excitement consumed me. Literally overnight, I went from a college student sleeping until noon to a motivated individual waking up at 7:00 AM every morning to check my download report from iTunes. Shortly thereafter, I started receiving email requests from users of my app asking me to include more features. I spent more long hours working to oblige those requests. Before long, I was devoting as many hours to programming as I was to my delivery job.

The process of listening to customer feedback and updating my app accordingly turned into a constantly repeating cycle. The days turned into months and before long, I had what could be considered a small business. Over the course of two years, I've learned a lot about the app market and I was honored when Taylor asked me to donate some of that knowledge to his new book. There are many lessons that I've learned over the past two years, but I feel that my friend Brian of Web Pyro, LLC summed it up best. He once told me, "Some of the complex issues that you run into when designing software are so crazy that they probably only have one in a million odds of ever occurring. The problem is that there are millions of them, so statistically you're bound to run into a few." He could not have been more right.

Although I feel that my career as a programmer is still just beginning and the experiences I have to draw on are limited, I have found several lessons to be near universal truths. The first of these truths is that working as an independent software developer provides you incredible freedom. You have the freedom to set your own hours and work how and when you please. Although it may feel like you are your own boss, you're not. Your customers are your boss and should always be treated that way.

The next word of advice I would pass on is that you can never expect to make everyone happy. It is an unachievable goal that you must always strive for, but no matter how vast of a resource pool you devote to your products and customer satisfaction, you will never please all of your customers. Handling these seemingly illogical consumers will be what defines your company's reputation for character and integrity.

Lastly, competition is not warfare. I carved out a niche for my business, and it has since become a crowded one. Although I strive to make the best products I can, I must respect the fact that there are others out there who will always come along and make similar (and admittedly sometimes better) features for their products. This is in fact how I met Taylor. We both designed similar products, but managed to learn from one another rather than undermine each other's efforts.

Competition, success, and failure are all part of the natural cycle of business and life. I am very thankful for the success that The

App Store has given me, but it is always important to know that success can depart as quickly as it arrives. For this reason, it is important to act with the understanding that nothing lasts forever and to enjoy any success you experience while it lasts, because only time will tell how lasting any given market truly is.

Brass Monkeigh explains some major points I want to emphasize. I am sure you have heard the saying "The customer is always right." This is beyond true for users. If you fail to keep your users happy, your apps will not do well. Brass Monkeigh saw a market opportunity and was able take advantage of this knowledge. He customized his apps to meet the needs of a particular segment. He is very humble, but let me tell you his latest line of apps are very well done and incorporate any possible feature a user can every imagine. Because of Brass Monkeigh's willingness to optimize features and content based on his customer base's requests, his apps have consistently ranked among the top 100 in the reference category for well over two years.

Let's apply this concept to your app. If you already have an app in The App Store, you probably woke up to download your sales expecting to be a millionaire; odds are this didn't happen. Maybe your lack of success is what has motivated you to read this book. If success has eluded you, it is not time to give up. Rather, it is time to analyze your app and come up with a good business model. The reason I have dedicated an entire chapter to niche and specialty apps is because of the competitiveness of The App Store today. The days of creating "fart" apps and fake scamming fingerprint scanners that make millions are over. Truthfully, I am glad they are over because I would get so infuriated when I would see these stupid apps making tons of money. People now expect quality, complex apps that focus on special interests and hobbies. If you're able create apps that enhance or integrate into a consumer's hobbies, you have struck gold.

- Picking the right app to develop

I cannot tell you how many clients come into my office each day and have this amazing idea for a game that is going to make billions. Usually I just shake my head. The gaming category of the app store is beyond competitive. If you create a game, your competitors, who are not indie developers but multi-millionaire companies, will have a significant advantage. I get this email about once a day "I want to create a game like *Angry Birds*." Really, you want to compete against an app that is so popular and branded, it now has shirts, toys, candy, and even headphones? Yeah, that will go well. Can you sense my sarcasm here?

Most novice appreneurs do not fully fathom the complexity involved in creating popular games. To compete alongside the games of this quality will require an investment of hundreds of thousands of dollars. For this reason, I deliver the same forewarning to clients who want to develop a game app. You will make a dollar or millions, and there isn't much room in between. I know scores of developers and appreneurs; many have made millions on apps, but none have made millions on games. I never shoot someone's dream down, but I try to let clients know that they are taking a huge gamble. Furthermore, the odds are stacked greatly against them. So to minimize the risk, I try to convince them of a smaller app for their first one. You need experience before taking on a project like that.

Perfection without practice is an unreasonable expectation with any endeavor and creating apps is no different. Therefore, I begin questioning my clients about hobbies and passions to help them with the app development process. Usually by the end of this conversation, they have nixed the idea of a game in favor of a niche app that will yield them more money and cost a fraction to develop. Though the gaming market has a small potential to be lucrative, the niche market shows more promise for long-term financial gain. Simple economics of supply and demand explains this phenomenon. The games market is flooded with choices; however, the niche market has fewer offerings for your target market. Needless to say, when consumers search for apps relevant to their particular hobby, the scarcity of choices will influence them to download those apps that appeal to their interests. It is a little known fact among experienced appreneurs that the specialized market is extremely popular and powerful. I'm not a fortune teller, but I could probably take your phone, look at the apps, and tell what your hobbies are.

- The power of niche and specialty applications

Advertising and marketing for niche apps is not difficult. For example, maybe you have created an app for bicyclists because you're an avid cyclist. Initially, you want to make sure when you market the app, only cyclists are exposed to the advertisement. There is no point in doing broad-spectrum ads such as Facebook or Google because not everyone cares about cycling. Free advertising is always the best, so begin accessing some forums for cyclists. Then, post about the app to let people know what you have made. It is likely the cycling groups will be excited to see what you have created. Next, look on YouTube for some popular cyclists. Remember, you have a new app, so don't approach Lance Armstrong or Dave Mirra. Instead, find popular but less known cyclists. Reach out to them, and see if they are willing to back and promote the app. You should expect to offer the cyclist sponsor something in return for the endorsement, either money or exposure. My experience has proven that having some popular You Tubers backing your app will be worth the aggravation; popularity sells.

After you have recruited popular cyclists to back your app, people on the forums will be talking about it. Next, it is time to approach some cycling companies for affiliate programs. Affiliate programs are set up to offer you money for selling their products. Companies offering these programs are also willing to advertise your app for you; of course, while they are advertising your interests, they are simultaneously advertising the company's products. By the completion of the affiliation process, your app is selling and you are making steady revenue. Consequently, people are buying your affiliate's products from the app, and you are making even more revenue. Affiliate programs are a well-kept secret in the app world that you now know about! The cycling example provides a model for successful app marketing. Even though you are not creating a bicycling app, changing this template to fit your app's needs is very simple.

In the world of niche apps, customer relations is of premium importance. People will want to contact you about your application.

This may be in the form of a bug report or just someone saying they enjoy the app. Be sure to include a simple email form in your app for these inquiries. Getting back to your customers in a timely fashion will benefit you significantly in the long run. You can build a great relationship with a user just by taking a few seconds to email them back. If your app is for users between the age groups of 12-18, this is even more important. Young consumers think it is so cool that the developer emailed them back and often look up to you. If your particular app is conducive to community interaction, take advantage of it. For instance, Brass Monkeigh makes guides for popular video games; he has one of the best customer relations models of anyone I know. He personally writes back the majority of his users' emails, and interacts with his users via Facebook and Twitter. His best form of customer interaction is community games. He invites his users to play the video games with him. By creating a connection with his consumers, he ensures that these people will download each app he makes, and believe me they do. People also share and retweet his apps constantly on the various social networks. So Brass Monkeigh has created a virtual relationship with his consumers ensuring repeat business and free advertising!

By taking time to build a relationship with your users, you are guaranteeing they will buy your future apps. These actions will make them feel like your friend; as a friend, they will likely advertise your apps to others. Remember to respect your customers. They paid money for your app, so keep them happy and add the features they want. The appreneurs that listen to their customers are always successful. It is now time to further your app education by learning about the various business models of apps.

Appreneurs

Chapter 4

"Generating revenue from various business models"

As you learn more about the world of apps, you begin to understand that different types of apps require different business models. Most amateur appreneurs think that the only way an application can generate revenue is the paid (pay a flat one-time fee to download the application, IE .99, 1.99, 2.99 etc.) model. While this is the simplest strategy, it doesn't always produce the results you desire. Over the last year, I have noticed that free apps with in app purchases, or freemium as appreneurs call them, have dominated the market. Here is why: people have no hesitation to download free apps. You will generally get between 50-100 free downloads per paid download. That means if fifty people downloaded your app for free, one would have paid outright for it. Now if this sounds like a very low number, that's because it is. The freemium model changes this up in your favor substantially. Please note, for the freemium model to work, you need to have an application that is enticing and entertaining. If your application is not something of value, why would a user buy premium upgrades? Let's take a quick tangent to illustrate this point. When you think of the apps that generate the most money, which ones come to mind? Possibly, you thought of *Angry Birds*, *Words With Friends,* or *Cut The Rope*? You might be surprised to know that all of the top five grossing apps are freemiums.

One of my freemium favorites, *Zynga Poker*, provides an excellent case study. This app is free for anyone to download. As you begin to play, you are provided a limited number of chips (virtual currency) with which to bet. Each day you play, you are awarded a few more chips. If you lose all of your daily chip allowance, how can you continue to play? In App Purchases, the game allows you to buy chips and continue playing. The game designers draw players in with the free app. They allow you to play the app and get "hooked." When you run out of chips, you have two choices: wait until tomorrow to play or pay a small fee to continue playing. Two personality traits that seem to be shared among app users is impulsivity and impatience; they HATE waiting! A wise appreneur can use this knowledge to his business advantage. Surely you are wondering who would pay for virtual currency that has no real value. I'll answer that for you, millions of people! Don't just take my word for it. Research the top 25 grossing apps (top grossing apps are the apps that produce the most revenue, not downloads) and see how many are freemiums with virtual currency or upgrades.

Another example, *Temple Run*, also took The App Store by storm. I downloaded it and played for a while, all the time wondering how does this app make any money? My first couple of exposures only showed it as a freemium. Then I saw it; as you progress through the levels, you earn coins to use on upgrades and unlocks. The game's design includes an in app purchase to acquire more coins. Once again I thought to myself, "Who would buy this? It has no purpose?" By the next day, I could answer my own questions because I was hooked on the game and wanted to upgrade my character. My decision was a simple one: I could play for a few hours and earn the coins, or spend a buck and buy them. I bought them and was actually quite happy with my purchase.

- Making money from free apps

Just because an app's price is free, doesn't mean it cannot make any money. The preceding case studies, *Temple Run* and *Zynga Poker*, provide excellent examples to disprove the notion that free apps are not profitable. Freemium apps are still one of the best ways to generate a large number of downloads, and then translate those downloads into good stable revenue. Remember, you will likely get between a 1:50 and a 1:100 paid to free download ratio. By being able to convert these massive amounts of free downloads into sales, you are going to likely make more money than even a paid only version. When I am creating a freemium app, I like to include ads and in app purchases. If you have a paid version of the game, do not feel guilty about adding ad banners to your free version. Ideally, you want to annoy someone with ads in the hope they will buy the paid version to remove them. Furthermore, I also try and offer an array of in app purchases. The more you can think of the better. You can have in app purchases to remove advertisements, add features, upgrade in app features, and much more. As stated in the discussion of freemium apps, you will be surprised of the things people will buy. Just because you find the idea of purchasing "virtual items" ridiculous, does not mean a user will share your perspective.

We have talked about both paid versions and freemium versions, so what is left? Free with ads is a business model that I would only suggest if there are no applicable in app purchases and a paid version doesn't make sense. This model allows you to have a completely free application with ads. These ads are your sole form of revenue. Therefore, the more users you have, the more money you will make on ads. In reality, appreneurs will not likely become millionaires from only ad revenue, but there is still money to be made.

The last business model is known as user base. A user base is essentially a collection of users that are engaged in the app. Most user bases contain a database with email addresses. In today's online world, user bases are worth their weight in gold. I'm sure you have heard of the free app *Instagram*. It seems unbelievable but true that *Instagram* has made over one billion dollars without presenting a single ad or in app purchase. In one famous business transaction, Facebook purchased *Instagram* primarily for its user base. This has happened more times than you would think in The App Store. Apps that require users to register will give appreneurs access to users' names and email addresses. This can become an invaluable business tool. If you build a good email list of your app's users, you can now market to them directly via email when you release a new app.

- Choosing the right business model

After considering all of the business model possibilities, which one will you choose for your apps? That answer should be fairly straightforward: all of them. Many of the top apps have both a paid version and a free version with ads and in app purchases. For what business reasons would they offer two choices? Exposure. Two versions doubles the chances that a user will find the app. The free with ads and in app purchase backed versions typically generate a greater number of downloads. Moreover, the more downloads you have, the more users you have; the more users you have, the more people are talking; the more people are talking, the more downloads you will get......... See the cycle here? To generate revenue, your app has to be downloaded. Ideally, your goal is to get users who downloaded the free version to upgrade to the paid version. Unfortunately, there is no guarantee that this transfer from free to paid will happen. Keep in mind, there are users that will never pay for an app; you will probably not sway their mindset regardless of what your app is or does. So how do you reach the users that are willing to pay? How do you convince them to download the paid version? If your app is a free game, I would use the following model: after each turn, show the user a full screen ad asking them to pay for the full version. If they click the ad, it should take them directly to The App Store to buy it. It will likely require multiple exposures to the advertisement to generate a sale, but if they play the game often, soon it will annoy them enough to purchase it. This method of advertisement exposure is a tactic commonly used by large companies. I actually saw this work with my girlfriend. She was playing one of the online games like *Scrabble*, and she was getting so annoyed with the ad coming up after each turn. Finally, I saw her digging in her purse for her credit card. I highly doubt she stopped playing to pay some bills.

Briefly I want to discuss how users in niche markets will pay more for apps. For this example, I will use an app I made that I will call *app X* (I leave my apps out of this book because I am not selling you a product, I am teaching you to make one). *App X* was a paid app ($2.99) that included premium features. I thought long and hard about what model I should use. The app was a paid only version and was generating good revenue. The users that bought the app absolutely loved it. I added the new premium features as a non-consumable (non-consumable in app purchases are bought one time and unlock new features or content) in app purchase. I really didn't expect the results I saw the next morning when I downloaded my sales report. I had a 78% conversion rate. That meant that 78% percent of the people that bought the app also bought the in app purchase. The lesson learned from this scenario is to not underestimate the power of premium features on a niche market. Just because users have already purchased your paid version, that does not mean they are unwilling to pay again. The opposite is actually true for one simple reason: people that are willing to pay for apps are exactly that, WILLING TO PAY! Make sure to take advantage of this, or you will be passing up a ton of potential revenue.

Since you now have gained insight to the variety of business models available, let's discuss the importance of managing your users.

Appreneurs

Chapter 5

" Managing users today for success tomorrow "

In the summer of 2011, I created a game app that I hoped would be a real success. After a few months of low sales, I decided to make the app freemium. With this new model, the game saw thousands of downloads each day. Server costs began to get pretty expensive and the app was taking up a lot of my time. Server costs are calculated generally by the amount of data your app's database uses. If you have an app that has a lot of database interactions and a lot of users your server costs can be hundreds a month. I wanted to move on to a new project, so I decided to sell the app. Although the app did not generate considerable revenue, it had a massive user base. I listed the app's rights for sale; the app sold within 48 hours. The interesting fact was that the buyer didn't buy the app because they liked it or because they saw it as a million dollar investment. They purchased it for one reason, the large user base.

Another little known fact to the majority of appreneurs is the worth of a good user base. Some of my success can be attributed to my early realization of this truth. If you neglect to capture your user base, you have a bunch of random users and no data to track. I advise clients to capture, or try to capture, a user's name and email. Collecting this data is relatively easy and can be done via a register screen and a simple database. If possible, it is beneficial to gather as much data as possible. In my apps, I capture the following fields of information:

Email

Username

Version Number

Paid or Free

Number of In App Purchases Bought

Online or Offline

Number of Emails Send (either to the developer or telling friends)

Number of in app Tweets or Facebook posts

To the inexperienced, these fields may appear to be too much information, but skilled appreneurs realize that information is power. The fact that database interactions are fairly inexpensive, make the data stored in them all the more valuable. If you are able to capture a ton of user data, you are going to be an expert about how users utilize your app. For instance, knowing how many people are online at an instance is a really valuable feature because you will know if a new update, or added feature, was a hit or miss. In the event that the time comes for you to sell the rights to the app, (we will talk more about this in depth in a later chapter) you will have all of this data at hand. As a result, you will have no problem selling the app. Investors love when apps have a good user base. They will want to know trends, daily active users, and if there is an email list associated with the app. The readily accessible answers to these questions will increase the likelihood that the investors will work out a great offer for you. Business investors will view you as a business professional who deserves respect. On the other hand, if you don't have data, you will appear unprepared and unworthy of a fair offer if they even decide to make any other at all.

- Capturing the right data for the right results

Capturing your user's information is just a part of a successful data retrieval plan. You need to be able to keep your users happy. Most importantly, you need to keep them using the app! I encourage clients to create a simple email address for their app. With an email address, you can allow users to contact you without ever leaving the application. I offer a few different options for emailing in my apps:

Feature Request – This allows users to email you their ideas for what could make the app better. I am sure you have heard the proverb "The customer is always right." This golden rule of business is the truth for your app's users as well. The best part of the feature request is that sometimes the best ideas come from the perspectives of your customers.

Bug Report – This allows users to tell you about any bugs and crashes they may experience. Generally, in your first version of the app there will be bugs. Taking heed to users' descriptions of glitches will allow you and your developer to improve the overall quality of your application. Adding this is a must.

Tell A Friend – By far, this is one of my favorite email features. Not many appreneurs use this feature, and why I will never know. I can only assume they think people will not actually use it. The truth is far different. One of our games gets over 100 Tell A Friend emails sent a day! I have a few suggestions on how to get similar results. First, pre-populate the body of the email with something like "I have been using APP NAME HERE, and it is a ton of fun. You need to check it out HTML DOWNLOAD LINK HERE". You can also CC yourself in the email, so that you get a copy each time this is sent. With this data feature, the user emails someone they know with this pre-defined email. The recipient opens the email (you will have close to a 100% open rate since the email is from someone they know well) and sees that the email talks about an awesome app. Immediately, they see "click to download" and tap it. The link directs them to The App Store to buy or download the app. Again, you have generated free advertising people!

Proof of this point is provided in visual below of the "Tell A Friend" email list and email body for my *Draw With Me* app:

:

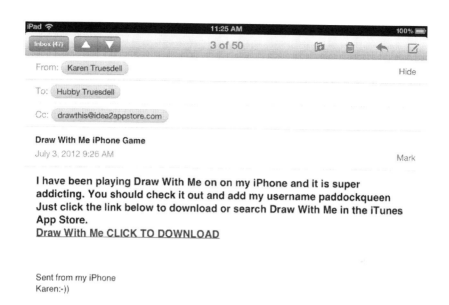

From: Karen Truesdell   Hide

To: Hubby Truesdell

Cc: drawthis@idea2appstore.com

Draw With Me iPhone Game

July 3, 2012 9:26 AM   Mark

I have been playing Draw With Me on on my iPhone and it is super addicting. You should check it out and add my username paddockqueen Just click the link below to download or search Draw With Me in the iTunes App Store.
Draw With Me CLICK TO DOWNLOAD

Sent from my iPhone
Karen:-))

As you see in the example above, there is a pre-populated Subject and Body. The body has the user's name, so the person they are inviting can play with them. I also include the download URL in addition to the app's title and how to search for it. The more information you can give for how to find the app, the better.

Rate The App – This isn't exactly an email, but it takes the user to The App Store to review the app. Reviews are more important than some appreneurs realize. Understanding the importance of reviews is one of my most treasured app store secrets. Reviews count towards your app store search number. The app store search number is where your app comes up for a searched term. I will outline this concept in more detail in an upcoming chapter. All you need to know for now is that the more reviews you have (they do not necessarily need to be good reviews), the higher you will rank for a searched term. For example, let's pretend you have an app with the title *APP Title – FUN APP*. Also, you have a competitor with a very similar title APP Title – *AWESOME APP*. Both of you have the word APP TITLE as the app's name followed by a subtitle. Further, you both have similar or the same key words. You even have the same number of downloads. Which app shows up first in the search? The deciding factor is the number of reviews. Knowing how reviews can give you an edge is a trade secret. Take advantage of your newfound knowledge.

- Social networks dos and don'ts

No instructions on how to manage users in the modern age would be complete without considering the proper integration of social networks. Although social networks might seem to be the ideal method to gain user data, my advice is DO NOT EVER require a user to sign in via a social network to use an app. There are apps that have lost over half of their user base because of imposing this requirement. Below are some reviews after a top 25 game made Facebook sign in mandatory. The reviews displayed are not modified or staged; it is a screenshot right from their reviews sections.

Allow the user to choose whether they want to use social

networks or not. If you are able to successfully integrate a social network, then you will be able to market to an exponential number of users. An explanation of why the social networking sites need to be tapped follows. If you neglect to use a social network, your users are limited to the linear form when they want to share your app. The linear form constraints only allow you to communicate with a few people at once, and most users won't even do that. Integrating a social network, allows hundreds of people to see your app for each person that posts to the social network, resulting in app exposure to an exponential number of potential users. For each post a user makes to the social network that refers to you app, most of his/her friends will see it on the newsfeed or timeline.

To illustrate the social network's capability, I will provide an example of a photo-sharing app. The user wants to share a picture via a social network. We need to do this in a way that advertises our app, but subtly. *Instagram*, for example, has mastered this subtle technique. For each picture shared on Facebook, they add a small image of their icon in the corner. The icon doesn't affect the quality of the picture and builds great brand recognition. In addition, they also add unique albums for the photos you upload from the app. To clarify how this exposure can help your app, evaluate what happens with each shared post. Our user just posted the photo to a social network. The user has 300 friends, most of whom saw the picture and the icon. A few of them were so intrigued, they downloaded the app. Now the new users have posted a picture, a few more friends download, and so on. This is how apps go viral. Exponential growth is very powerful; you need to take advantage of it and the free advertising it allows. Ignoring the possibilities social networking sites provide is forfeiting the chance that your app will go viral. Plain and simple, the more people that see your app, the better chances you have of it being successful. Social networks are all about fads. If something is viewed as the latest hot toy, people will not hesitate to download it.

Keeping your users happy is crucial for long-term app success. Maintaining user satisfaction will encourage your users to continue purchasing your apps in addition to advertising your apps to their friends. Implement these tips in your application development, and I believe there is a good chance I will be reading about your app one day. In the next chapter, I will provide a guide on determining what apps are hot and what apps are not.

Appreneurs

Chapter 6

"What's hot and what's not"

One trait that has allowed me to become successful as an appreneur is my ability to generate ideas for apps. Granted I am a very creative individual, but there is more to it than that. I have learned how to quickly and effectively find out what apps are selling and what apps are not. Researching the latest apps isn't as complicated as some people make it out to be. In fact, the only tool you will ever need is your smartphone or tablet. I have discovered that the best way to come up with apps is to get out of your office and focus on your hobby. I am a car enthusiast, so when I need to come up with ideas or get away from it all, I take a drive. A good half of the apps I have brainstormed have originated while taking my car out for a spin on my favorite road. My experience has been that once the appreneur bug bites, it is hard to stop thinking about app possibilities.

- Using the app store to make apps

Even the most creative minds become plagued by app creation block occasionally. So when you are struggling to invent new ideas, where can you look for inspiration? Since the best new ideas are often inspired by old ideas, the answer is so simple: The App Store. Because of The App Store's structure, you can literally see which apps are selling and which apps are not. Make the reading of The App Store's top selling apps part of your daily routine to ensure long-term success, much like traditional businessmen faithfully read the stock reports. Wake up and first check your app sales. Next, browse each category's top 100 apps. Here you will see the most popular selling apps, an invaluable tool overlooked by novice appreneurs. I have clients come in daily asking, "Do you think this app will do well?" I open up my phone and find something similar (if applicable). By using the rankings of a similar app, I can give them a rough estimate of what the app is making per day. After browsing these categories, take a look at the top 200 overall paid apps. Most of these are large companies that are hard for independent developers to compete against. Keep an eye out for developer names you don't recognize. If you see a new app that has broken the top 200 and is not produced by a major company, you are looking at a new hot market. Your diligence in recognizing new markets will provide you with intuition about which markets are doing well. With this information, you can consider making an app that is better or similar to this popular app. Do not hesitate long if you hope to capitalize on the success of a hot new market. These types of markets are time sensitive. You need to be able to get an app out to The App Store fast, and having a good developer is a key component to speed. True, good developers may cost more, but they are generally much faster.

Steve Jobs once said, "Good artists copy, great artists steal." If you want to compete in these hot, or fad, market apps, you need to be able to not only clone the successful parts of the new app, but also expand on the app's capabilities. To do this, you need to download their app and use it. Just as discussed in chapter one, you need to do your research. Think about what makes this app popular. What are the users saying in reviews? Now for the big question, what can I do better? If the answer is nothing, DO NOT WASTE YOUR TIME AND MONEY! Conversely, if you know there is something you can do better, it is time to hit the ground running. You need to implement these improved features and the app very quickly. Each day you wait is a day your competitor further captures the market. At times these replicated apps can be a gamble, but they can pay off very well. Compared to other app markets, these apps will not provide years of long-term stable revenue, but you can make a lot of money fast by finding creative inspiration in existing apps. Don't forget to see if *http://www.appcod.es* has your competitor's app's keywords, so you can know what they are using and put yourself even further ahead.

- 'Tis the season to make apps

Seasonal apps, like the hot and fad apps discussed in the section above, are time sensitive. Although these apps have a limited sales period, some have been popular enough to rank among the top 100 sellers overall. Examples of seasonal apps range anywhere from countdowns to important dates, holiday cartoons for kids, Santa trackers; the possibilities are as endless as your creativity and your ability to market for the appropriate season. Although these apps only sell for a short term, they can produce quick revenue.

The season I like to focus on is Christmas. The Christmas season is the golden time of the year for an appreneur. My first Christmas in The App Store I made $1211 in sales on Christmas day alone. Keep in mind, the week prior I was only averaging about $80 a day. Considering those Christmas sales were during my first year in The App Store, I was fortunate to be able to gain valuable knowledge so early in my developing career. Here is why Christmas is such a powerful sales season for us appreneurs. You have kids receiving iPhones/iPads/iPods as gifts; they will usually get an iTunes card for the device as well. They will be more than devoted, even compelled, to spend every dime on this card in a matter of seconds. The ideal demographic for Christmas sales is children between the ages of 10-18. Because the age demographic is so broad, appreneurs have creative freedom in appealing to the diverse interests of this broad spectrum of ages.

One app that really did well last year was a virtual Santa tracker. Hats off to the guy that made this; he is a marketing genius. I had been tracking his sales for the week prior to Christmas. He was ranked about 198 overall, which is amazing for any appreneur. When Christmas Eve arrived, he had managed to jump to number 21! I'm certain this phenomenal jump in sales allowed him to buy a really nice present for himself. Seasonal apps are all about being in the right market at the right time. Finding popular seasonal apps can be done in the same fashion as mentioned above. A word of forewarning though about seasonal apps, give yourself at least a month before the peak holiday season to generate sales. In other words, if you have a cool Christmas app, you need to have it in The App Store by Thanksgiving. Do not plan on submitting the app Christmas Eve.

- A new idea for a new market

An increasingly unique situation might be that your app idea is not represented at all in The App Store. What does this mean? There are a few things this can mean: some are good and some are bad. The first thing you need to do in this situation is talk with an experienced developer (make sure you have an NDA signed). Check to make sure your idea is a technical possibility and something your respective app store will allow. If your app checks out for both of these areas, then you are in a gambling position. The app may either do really well or really poorly. How popular is the community for the app you are planning developing? If the answer is small, then chances are the app may not do well. On the other hand, if the community is fairly large, you could very well be sitting on a gold mine.

Just because there are hundreds of thousands of apps in The App Store doesn't mean all of the good ideas are taken. New breakthrough apps hit the store every day, and this will continue for years to come. The more creative you are the better. I have created a few apps for clients where I sat in my office thinking to myself, is there even remotely a market for this? The answer was yes. One of these surprisingly successful apps was an interactive wildlife guide. Basically their app provides information on anything you would need to know to identify a bug, plant, or animal in the wild. For the bulk of adults, this kind of app sounds like something the majority of people would never download and that is a reasonable assertion; however, there are enough enthusiasts to keep these apps in the top 25 of the Reference category.

By keeping an eye on app trends and fads, you'll be able to predict and understand the app market. When you're able to successfully do this, you will notice your sales begin to climb. In time, you will even be able to accurately estimate what an app may make.

Appreneurs

Chapter 7

"Making the most of your advertising money"

      Experience has been my teacher concerning advertising apps. I wish I could say that I nailed it on my first try, or second, or even third. Thankfully, I know how to learn from my mistakes, because I have made every advertising mistake one could before I learned how to do it effectively. One seemingly sound source of advertisement advice is ad agencies. They will likely contact you with these ad campaigns that are too good to be true. I fell for these a few times. I ran a massive campaign with one of these agencies and saw no increase in sales. I wasted thousands of dollars; I can tell you that it leaves a really bad taste in your mouth. After hearing from all of the fellow developers and appreneurs over the years that made the same mistakes, I am a little less embarrassed. By reading this book, I hope you can learn from our mistakes and don't have to go down the same path. Hopefully, you can learn from my experiences to run successful advertising for your app on the first try!

      Before we talk about what works for advertising, I want to make you aware of the failures I, along with other appreneurs, have made. One of the ad campaigns I quickly learned doesn't work for the app market is Facebook. They offer very inexpensive ads, but the truth is no one clicks them. I imagine most people just tune them out. Because the majority of Facebook users use the mobile app, which doesn't serve any ads, app advertisement is missed by the largest part of Facebook's audience. I have yet to meet a developer that has had success with the Facebook ad model, and I highly doubt I ever will. The issue you have with cost per click ads and apps is when someone clicks your app's ad, and remember this can only happen from the desktop version of the site, they will likely be directed to your app's website or app store URL. From here the user must then grab their phone and search the app name to download. I can assure you, this rarely happens. This business model works well with websites that wish to gain more traffic, but is just horrible for apps. If you use an impression model with Facebook, you will face the same issues. Unless your app's ad literally screams at the user, they probably will never see it. If they do click it, we are back at the issue stated above.

Recall Chapter 4's discussion of integration of social networks within apps. This is the most effective method to advertise on Facebook; best of all it is free and works on mobile devices. I am a big fan of free advertising, as you will soon learn, and have found ways to market apps without spending a fortune.

The next advertising failure is banner ads. Granted they are more productive than Facebook ads, yet they still will produce minimal results and you are likely to not break even. I have tried advertising apps on a wide array of websites. In one of my many failed banner ad ventures, I ran an ad on a popular app reviewing website hoping to get great results. To my chagrin, even the popularity and content of the site, did not increase my sales. Take a look at my results:

255,862 impressions

117 clicks

0.05% click through rate

I paid almost 400 dollars for the ad and noticed no increase in sales. Obviously, banner ads were not worth the expense invested. This type of ad was also one of the ads recommended by a "big" ad agency. The issue with these agencies is that they are salesmen. They are not trying to make your app do better; they are trying to sell you something.

- Advertising methods that work

The failures would not be easy to share if I couldn't also share the good advertising moves I have learned. This may sound a bit unconventional, but Twitter blasts are becoming a good direct form of advertising. I ran a few of these and had some great results. Best of all they are super cheap! Here are some stats from one I ran the same time as the banner ad mentioned above.

Now the number of impressions is a little harder to gauge with

Tweets. For this I am going to assume all of the 9000 followers saw the tweet, which isn't the case but just humor me.

9000 impressions

161 clicks

1.8% click through ratio

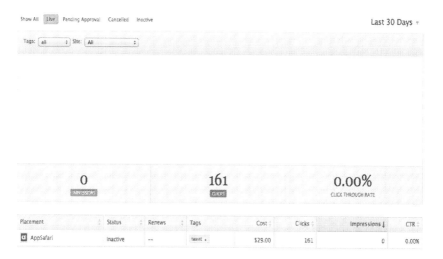

From an advertising standpoint, the percentage shown is a low click through ratio. I am fairly sure not all of the followers saw the tweet. I did, however, notice approximately 80 more downloads that day. At a mere cost of only $30, the tweet was a beneficial advertising choice. There are a lot of these packages found on various advertising websites or from the Twitter account holder directly. If you compare the results, the Twitter ad was considerably cheaper with far superior results.

Targeted Tweets/Facebook Blasts are especially productive advertising tools with specialty apps. If you have a niche app as mentioned in Chapter 1, focusing on the market population that is encompassed by your niche will make advertising more effective. I would stay away from the mass Tweets mentioned above and try and find people that are useful or in the same niche as your app to make the Tweets. Although enlisting a niche celebrity to create the Tweets may cost more, the results yielded will be substantial. With this method, you'll experience the best results because your market is targeted: the majority of the people that follow the person you are pursuing for the Tweet are fans of the same niche your app targets. Is the power of niche apps beginning to sink in? By working directly with popular people in your niche, you will be able to work out new and innovative methods of advertising that can help your app reach its full potential.

- The power of YouTube

YouTube is a very influential form of advertising that many appreneurs just refuse to use. I am not talking about the ads before a video or the ads that appear in the corner of the screen; instead, I propose using videos as ads. The more video ads you have, the better. I have yet to see a video on YouTube with 0 views. Realistically, I can't find a video as I am writing this with less than 500 views. Since I love free advertising, I find it wasteful to not capitalize on the free YouTube advertising market. Make a YouTube account if you do not have one. Make an account for your app, your development studio, even your cat's name; it doesn't matter. YouTube allows you to have as many accounts as you want. If you choose to make multiple videos of your app, be sure and use a different title and keywords for each video. You don't want to appear to be someone who is just spamming YouTube with videos. Change them up a bit, and you will be fine. Next, contact a few of the big YouTube app review channels. *CrazyMikesApps,*

UniqueApps, *AppStoreReviewer*, *TechTechManTV*, *Appolicious*, and *AppVee*, are all good ones to reach out to. They will likely take a while to get back to you, but if they do try and get a video review. This can cost you between $150 and $500, but it is money well spent. They have hundreds of thousands of subscribers, and these subscribers look up to these reviewers like gods. If they review the app favorably, their subscribers will buy it. Finally, try to enlist a few people that are popular in the niche and have a video done. Refer to Chapter 1 for tips on how to do this.

Although I have not had success with large advertising agencies in general, there are a few marketing firms out there that can produce successful results. Something to note is that these guys do not come cheap. You aren't paying for their time, you are paying for their contacts, and believe me they have some good ones. One company I recently used was *http://appspire.me/*. These guys really know their business, and they have some amazing promotional contacts. What they do is make sure your app gets visibility, and in the ways I have mentioned above. They will send press release info to the media, review websites, and YouTube reviewers. They will also do Facebook and Twitter blasts for you. They specialize in advertising your app during the different life cycles, which is a huge plus. They can handle everything from pre-launch, launch, and post launch. If you have an app that you think has the potential to be the next big app, I would highly recommend trying a marketing firm.

- App to app advertising

App to app advertising is a unique form of advertising, but it is also very effective. App to app advertising is where you show a list of your other applications inside of your app. The reason this method of advertising is so effective is that you have already proven the quality of your applications to the consumer. An example of the logistics of the process follows. A user has downloaded one of your apps; it would be reasonable to assume that if they like it, they will have no problem downloading other apps you have created. There are two ways to do this, simple and designed. Simple is just a line of code that when tapped directs the user to The App Store with a pre-defined search for your publisher name. The simple plan works well if you don't have any one "squatting" on your name (using your publisher name as keywords in their app to gain publicity). For this reason, I like to design my own "My Apps Screen." This can be done to either mimic the look and feel of the app store or something completely different; it all boils down to how creative you can be. Following the same advice given for screenshot design, you should remember that creative ideas need to be executed professionally. The last thing you want is someone not checking out your other apps because your page looks poorly designed or is hard to navigate. If you are ever unsure of the execution of a design choice, stick to the plain style.

- Advertising your app in other apps

There are basically two methods of utilizing other apps for advertising purposes. Option one is to contact a developer of a popular app who is willing to allow your app advertisement within theirs. This type of arrangement will likely cost a fair sum of money, but it can achieve fantastic results. A second option is a service called *Tap for Tap* (_www.tapfortap.com_). *Tap for Tap* is a unique form of advertising. Essentially you install their SDK in your app, and it will show other developers apps within your app as an ad banner. Each time this is done, you earn credits; these credits will then allow you to advertise your app in the same manner on other developers' apps. Using this service is an excellent opportunity to garner exposure for your app without excessive expense.

- Cross promoting user bases

Cross promoting user bases is essentially utilizing networking contacts. Through your adventures as an appreneur, you will likely meet other appreneurs who have great apps that do not compete directly with yours. You may approach them and propose an advertising trade agreement: you can advertise to their user base and in return you will advertise them to yours. Again, cross promoting provides another free advertising opportunity that typically yields excellent results. I have done this a few times over the years and found it to be one of the better forms of advertising. To foster a mutually beneficial advertising relationship, you must choose carefully the right person or app for cross promotion. I am a firm believer in the motto "It's not what you know, it's who you know." Consequently, if I find an app that I like, I try and reach out to the appreneur and let them know I, as an appreneur, enjoyed their app. To me, it is the highest form of compliment when another professional within the craft extends appreciation for your work. In most of my personal cases, I'll then carry on to maybe talk about one of my apps or anything that can start a good conversation. By the end of the email conversations, I usually have a new appreneur friend. As a matter of fact, this is how I met most of the people whose stories you have read in this book. Branch out; don't be shy and sheltered. Most appreneurs are just like you and love meeting new people. You also have something in common: you both sell apps! No matter how much you think you know, there is always someone that knows more. Find the experts, cross promote your apps with them, and learn from them.

To maximize your app's popularity, exhaust the recommended advertising markets: videos on YouTube, Facebook (as integrated into your app, NOT FACEBOOK ADS), and Tweets. Then, wait a few days and run a Google search on your app's name. Because of your advertising diligence, you will likely have more results other than the standard app store URL. This is the type of result you want to see. The more results that appear in your search, the more web traffic your app is generating. Ideally this data will also reflect an increase in sales, so now you can pat yourself on the back. You have just successfully advertised and marketed an app with low risk and expense.

Appreneurs

Chapter 8

"Plan to scale or your app will fail"

The first big success I had in an app was an interactive guide for the popular video game *Halo 3*. Since I was a fairly amateur appreneur and developer, I needed app content that was relatively simple. The app market was already stocked with guide apps, so I needed to make mine better. I partnered with one of the top pro gaming teams Optic Gaming and Kontrol Freek and had them advertising the app in a lot of different ways: they would run ads on their YouTube channels, post on their Facebook and Twitter, talk about the apps at events, and email their followers. This was a fantastic way for me to maximize my exposure with absolutely no out of pocket costs. Of course not every app will allow this scenario, but if you think outside the box, you can always come up with unique marketing techniques. The app reaped great results: number 2 in reference and number 188 overall! I had tens of thousands of users, and for an app in a market this specific it was about as viral as it could be. I did everything in my power to keep my users happy and engaged. I was able to keep this app at the top for almost a year. Of the scores of lessons I learned from this app's success, how to handle the viral potential of an app was to be the most crucial.

Going viral is when something becomes immensely popular at an exceedingly fast rate. In the app world, viral apps are a developer's dream because of the huge profit margins gained. However, as an amateur appreneur if you do not understand what to expect and how to prepare for this good fortune, you may not reap all of the benefits possible. You will need to plan for this in the beginning by devising strategies to handle the immense amount of downloads. I neglected to do this on a game I made, and it sure came back to bite me. In the spring of 2012 *Draw Something* took The App Store by storm, you literally couldn't open a blog or e-news article without reading about it. I decided to have my team at www.idea2appstore.com develop our spin off of the game. Everything went smoothly, and we had a nice working version in about two months. In chapter 5, I warned against requiring your users to login via Facebook. The following opportunity was provided to me because not all app developers think the same way. A few weeks after Zynga purchased *Draw Something*, I saw that they were now requiring Facebook login to play. I was amped! Normally, my development team doesn't even bother going up against the big companies, but this opportunity was huge. I opened up The App Store and took a look at the reviews for *Draw Something*. Just as I had expected, they were getting slammed with one star reviews by annoyed users. This was our opportunity, something I had dreamed about for years. Before we continue with the story, I want to point out a difficult lesson I learned from this adventure. If you have an app that uses a database, buy quality hosting. Sadly, I did not do this, and since I don't want to be accused of libeling anyone, I will leave the guilty party unnamed. Basically the company offered dirt-cheap hosting, which was something we initially saw as a good move since the game we made sends and receives tons of data. Assuming we only had a few hundred users, our hosting choice would have been a nonissue; instead, we had tens of thousands of daily active users within a few hours. I was so excited... until I played the game. Everything was timing out; basically, the puny virtual servers couldn't handle the load. I was beyond upset. In retrospect, I really should have planned that going viral was a possibility instead of trying to save a few bucks. The game is now hosted on a dedicated server and has no issues; unfortunately, it was too little too late. Our opportunity to take down a big name had passed. A positive aspect of this missed opportunity is that I am able to pass on my valuable lesson learned to you today.

- Tracking trends and producing results

You need to keep an eye on your trends. As you start to see a rise in downloads, you need to prepare yourself. Not all apps have servers and databases, but that is just a minor part in the overall scheme. In this next example, we will examine an app that doesn't have a server, database, or interactions. Before you get too excited about the prospect of low maintenance apps equaling no responsibility, let me correct your thinking. With a large influx of users, you are going to be bombarded with emails, Twitter and Facebook posts, and publicity. To the inexperienced, it may sound like no big deal, but it is super stressful and overwhelming at times. The added responsibilities will test your time management skills. Besides the added publicity and inquiries from reviewers, you will still need to interact with your community in whatever way you can. Be sure and continue your communications with any users asking questions via email. If you neglect this commitment to users, your app will not be popular for long. A key component of business longevity still applies: if you are able to keep your users happy, your application will continue to trend upward. Once users feel neglected and interest wanes, your app will inevitably trend down.

Tracking trends is a requirement for any successful appreneur. Fortunately, there are a variety of tools available for tracking necessary app data. Expect a short-lived appreneur career if you think tracking trends consists only of logging in and downloading sales. Some categories you need to track as an appreneur are the following:

Downloads/ Sales – This is fairly self-explanatory. You need to know how many people either purchased or downloaded your app.

Ranking – This is the rank of your app in its respective category. Rank is determined by the number of sales or downloads. These numbers will fluctuate daily. Keeping a close eye on rank will let you know if any new changes you have made are working in your favor.

Reviews – The review system is a bit flawed. Generally happy users don't leave reviews as often as unhappy users. If you are getting bad reviews, take note of what the user has to say. You will always get users leaving one star reviews saying "bad app" or "stupid app." Generally speaking, these are comments generated by competitors. You can always submit these reviews to your respective app store and have them removed. To do this, simply contact Apple with your app's name and App ID and request the review be removed. They are usually pretty good about taking care of this issue. You should pay attention if you see a few one star reviews pointing out the same issue, and quickly address any problems.

Keyword Search Ranking – This is similar to the download ranking mentioned above; however, it is purely based on how your app stacks up for searched terms. The majority of the users that download your app will have searched a particular term to find it. Knowing what number you come up for a search term is valuable information. I will cover how to effectively track this data in a moment.

Featured In App Store – If your app is doing well, there is a chance it can come up in the Featured What's Hot or New and Noteworthy sections of The App Store. These are all major accomplishments, and if your app gets one of these take a second to congratulate yourself. Usually, you will only be able to track this manually for your country of residence. Remember, The App Store reaches over 150 countries, each of which have their own rankings and featured sections.

Featured On The Web – Many websites feature and review apps. In the fortuitous event that your app becomes featured on one of these sites, you will see a sizable jump in downloads. You need to know if and when your app has been featured on these sites. From what I have found, there is not a better tool than a simple Google search for this. Search your app's title and run through about 4 pages of results. If your app is not listed, then you know your app has not yet been featured.

Manually tracking the sheer magnitude of data available to

track your app is literally impossible. Lucky for you, my appreneur experiences have led me to discover some awesome tools to help you do this. Best of all, most of them are free, and the ones that are not are well worth the investment.

- Tools for tracking downloads

AppViz - http://www.ideaswarm.com/AppViz2.html

AppViz is a tool I have been using since I first started selling apps. It is a powerhouse for collecting data. It provides you with the following results:

Rankings

Downloads/ Sales

Reviews

It keeps all of your data in one place and allows you to create graphs. Especially helpful for tax purposes, it quickly figures out weekly, monthly, or yearly sales. Additionally, it keeps track of your rankings in all of the countries and even translates your out of country reviews for you. *AppViz* will run you $49 dollars, but, like I said, it is well worth every penny.

Distimo – http://www.distimo.com/

Distimo is a very easy to use tool to track your daily, weekly, and monthly sales. All you have to do is register your account with their website, and you will receive an email each morning with your sales numbers. They have a really approachable interface for this, and I highly recommend them. Unlike some tools, it is completely free and takes no time to set up and use.

AppSales Mobile - https://github.com/omz/AppSales-Mobile/

AppSales Mobile is an open source app that you can download and install on your device. You will need the most recent copy of Xcode to make this work. Most developers will handle installation of this app on your device if you make the request. This app is probably one of my favorites. It is super easy to use and lightning fast. You can track downloads/sales by country or app. Just like *AppViz*, it collects all of your reviews and translates them. This app allows you to view daily, weekly, and monthly sales. Another cool feature is how the data is displayed: color coded bar graphs for each individual app, just like *AppViz*. Color coding provides you with a clear visual of which of your apps are selling well and which ones are not. *AppSales Mobile* is also free!

- Tools for tracking app store ranking

App Annie - http://www.appannie.com/

App Annie is one of my favorite tools for tracking app ranking. They provide a wealth of useful data. One of the many powers of *App Annie* is the ability to track competitor's rankings. The site is very simple to use; all you do is search by app or publisher name, and you can see current and past rankings. Because of the valuable data and ease of navigation, it is difficult to believe it has the added bonus of being free!

MajicRank - http://majicjungle.com/majicrank.html

MajicRank is a unique app because it is the only one I have found that allows you to track the real time current ranking. Most sites like *App Annie* lag behind about 24 hours. *MagicRank* pulls its data in real time. You can also track competitors, but you have to have their app ID. To obtain the app ID, simply run a Google search on the app's name and copy the ID from the app store URL like show below.

Here is one of my apps:

http://itunes.apple.com/us/app/caption-me/id528817199?mt=8

The highlighted portion is the app ID. All you need to do now is plug the app ID into *MajicRank,* and you now have real time ranking of any competitor's app you choose. An added bonus is that *MajicRank* is free to download and use!

- Tools for tracking keyword rankings

AppCodes - http://www.appcod.es/

My recent discovery of *www.appcod.es* a few months ago has definitely been a helpful data tracking source. This site offers some of the best search engine optimization available for apps. It allows you to track your competitor's keywords, which is very important information to know. Also, they have some unique features for keyword optimizing. They allow you to test keywords, and they will let you know what position your app rank accordingly. Because keywords are so integral to app sales, this feature provides invaluable information, which can be a deciding factor in your app's success. www.*appcod.es* is only $14.95 a month, and for the services they offer, it is a bargain.

Search Man SEO - http://www.searchman.com

 Search Man SEO is another valuable tool I have found. If used in combination with *appcod.es*, you will be able to dominate the keyword market. *Search Man* tracks all of your keyword rankings for you and any competitors you choose. As you will find out, keyword rankings are similar to download rankings in that they fluctuate greatly. Knowing where you stand each day is crucial from a marketing standpoint. You will receive a very user-friendly email each day around lunchtime. The email update will contain detailed information regarding your app's keywords. Preemptively, they also track new potential competitors for you based on keywords. *Search Man SEO* costs $20 per app monthly. To ensure your satisfaction, they also offer a trial version, so you can become comfortable with the product before buying.

 Of all the data responsibilities, tracking keywords is probably the most tedious task. It doesn't help that Apple is notorious for changing the search algorithm with no advance warning. Consequently, I try and check my keywords daily to make sure nothing has happened that could cause my apps not to show up in the rankings. The moment I notice an app's drop in rankings, I respond by either advertising more to push it back up the ranking, or I choose a new keyword. Remember, if users cannot find your app, they cannot download it.

 The sheer numbers of tools available for data tracking might be overwhelming. You will probably question which you should use. The answer to this hypothetical question is ALL of them. There is no one tool that does everything. Each one mentioned above offers something of use that the other does not. Use them all in harmony, and you will be satisfied with the results. The next topic of interest to a successful appreneur is the life cycle of apps.

Appreneurs

Chapter 9

"The life cycles of apps"

     Much like a living entity, apps have an expected expiration date for success, or what I like to refer to as a life cycle. To complicate matters, no two apps have the same life cycle. With all of the information presented to this point, it should be easy for you to predict where you app is in terms of its life cycle. A flawed assumption made by some people is that if you make a popular app, it will sell at the top forever. This is not true even with the top selling games. *Angry Birds* provides an excellent example. When this app is trending downward, the experienced developers make a new iteration of the game or launch a major update to counteract the downward trend. If they did not make these changes, in all likelihood, they wouldn't even be in the top 200 today. Not all apps have the same time frame when it comes to cycles, but they all generally trend the same. Understanding trends requires you to acknowledge The App Store's three unique seasons: pre-holiday season (September-November), holiday or peak season, (December-February), and slow season (March – August). An unwise appreneur will only look at sales numbers (the amount of money they are making) to determine trends and cycles, but it is imperative that you consider all of the information at hand to make the best decisions for your app.

- Tracking the right data

The only effective way to track your app's trends and life cycle is by app store ranking. The reason is that during the different app seasons, the volume of apps varies greatly. For example, if you have a top 200 app during the holiday season, you will see around 750 paid downloads. Conversely, during the slow season this number can be as low as 500. If you were tracking your app purely on revenue, you might logically assume your app is trending down; however, it is not. Keeping a close eye on ranking provides the most accurate data when tracking app's cycles.

- App launch life cycle

When you first release your app, you will likely trend upward that entire week. Your app is automatically featured in The App Store's "New" category for the first few days. Additionally, many third party sites will scrape (pull data) from The App Store to showcase; therefore, your app will likely show up in some *Google* searches as well. Statistically, your new release trend will reach an apex 4-5 days after your app has been released. What you do next will determine if you continue to stay at the top or plummet to the bottom.

- Post launch life cycle

If you have applied all of the strategies thus far, your app is doing well. You are reading your reviews, tracking rankings and other important data. To remain viable in the app market, it is now time to start thinking about how you can add or improve features. Leonardo Da Vinci said, "Art is never finished, only abandoned." This is my favorite quote to illustrate the habitual mistake amateur appreneurs make with their first few apps. They abandon them; they think just because the app is launched in The App Store and doing well, they can rest on their proverbial "laurels," getting paid forever. Unfortunately the misconception of The App Store being a "get rich quick", "easy" way to riches has been perpetuated by many authors and bloggers who have misled the general public. The truth is the opposite; it is a job like any other. If you start a successful soft drink company and never go to work after the first day, how long do you think the company will keep making a profit? I tested this theory with an app not long ago. A few days after the app ranked among The App Store's top 200 overall, I decided to see how long I could ride the wave. In January, the app was producing over $1000 dollars a day. I didn't maintain contact with my community of users or add any updates. Even today the app is still in version one, so I could test my theory. Not surprisingly, I was correct in my hypothesis. After only two months, sales plummeted. Today (June 21st, 2012), the app made a paltry $8. Simply put, if you do not continue to work with your apps and customers, you will eventually trend down into the dirt. To avoid the aforementioned scenario, take note of the secrets and tips I have learned.

- Updating apps to keep users engaged

In Chapter 1, I commented that users love updates. This should be imprinted into your brain by now. Updates are the single best way of keeping your application from trending downward. Types of updates can vary from huge new features to simple bug fixes. As long as you are doing your best to keep your users happy, they will continue to download and use the app. If you let your app become stagnant and boring, your users will leave and never come back. Usually when a user becomes bored with an app, they delete it. To avoid deletion disaster, you must keep your current users using the app. There are a few ways to do this:

Push Notifications – Push Notifications are messages sent to your users from the app. The cool fact about the power of Push Notifications is they have close to a 100% open rate. Because they pop up on the main screen of a user's phone, they are difficult to ignore. Use these sparingly; the last thing you want to do is spam your users. I generally send them when I add a new update.

Email Notifications – If you have a good email list for your users, you can send the same types of notifications via email. Unlike push notifications, emails are not opened as often; in addition, you may anger some users who view these notifications as junk mail. I only use this method if I don't have an app with push notifications.

Social Network Pages – Make sure and chime in on your social network pages. Let your users know you are listening and working on the app. Feel free to use your own app and post some of your own content. Users love to see the developer using the app.

Facebook/Twitter Posts – Be sure and utilize the social media outlets associated with your app. These are fantastic ways to interact with your users. I usually make posts when a new feature has gone into development, when it is submitted to the app store, and when the update is live for download. This will keep your users up to date, and in a sense include them in the development process.

- Generating new sales

Besides maintaining your current user base, any wise business plan will also include new customer generation. To generate new sales, you should continue to advertise as mentioned in Chapter 6. Advertising is not a one-time project; follow the same quote as above "Advertising is never finished, only abandoned." To keep your app business fresh, make sure you always have ads, videos, and promos going live. Most of these advertisement categories will run for an allotted time, so make sure you don't let them all expire. Inexperienced appreneurs typically make the mistake of only running one ad campaign. Can you imagine what would happen if major companies did this? My guess is that they wouldn't be major companies for long. Continue to find new and innovative ways to advertise your application, and you will always be ahead of your competition. As The App Store continues to grow, those who can effectively advertise and market will come out on top.

Seasonal iterations of apps can be a huge sales boost. Observe The App Store around Christmas; usually, some of the most popular apps have a Christmas version. Typically, only the big companies do this, but more indie appreneurs need to be informed. Adding a new version of your app with a Christmas or Halloween theme to it can drive your sales up exponentially. *Angry Birds* did this with their *Angry Birds* seasonal game. It is the same game with a few new levels and a Christmas theme. The seasonal version also turned a considerable profit; users did not mind paying again for basically the same app.

Partnering with new affiliates can also be a good way to make a new version of the app. Imangi Studios, the creators of *Temple Run*, provide an excellent example to follow. They created a similar version of the game that featured characters from the movie *Brave*. Their original game had been trending down for the last few months; however, as soon as the *Brave* movie version of *Temple Run* hit the store, they were back at the top.

Sometimes you need to think "outside the box" to keep your apps from trending down. There is no defined way to accomplish this, but by following these tricks you will have exhausted all of your efforts. Just remember this, if you abandon your app, your users will abandon you.

Appreneurs

Chapter 10

"Selling the rights and cashing out"

You have undoubtedly heard of people selling successful businesses, making millions, and instantly retiring. Apps are no different. With the market growing the way it is, investors are always looking for new apps to buy. Because the app market is so young, buyers will pay top dollar for rights. The instances I have sold the rights to apps have been fortunate circumstances that netted me lucrative profits. When I have wanted to take on a new project or adventure, selling a particular app's rights has provided me with both the capital and freedom to pursue other options. No matter what the app is, there is always a buyer out there. I know some appreneurs that have retired at a very young age by simply selling the rights to their app at the perfect time.

Since a new market has emerged in the last year from buying and selling the rights of apps, it is important that you know the process and expectations. In the event that a buyer wants to buy the rights to your app, this will include and is not limited to, source code, user base, future revenues, and development team. Think of someone wanting to purchase the rights to your app like someone buying a website domain. Basically, once the transaction is complete, the app is no longer yours. You may question why you would ever want to give up your creative work, but you will also learn quickly that once the app bug bites, it is hard to limit your app creation. Likely, you will start with one app, and then quickly make another. The creative process will continue, and before you know it, you will have a plethora of apps. Having multiple apps is a great business model for sustained revenue, but it is also very time consuming and stressful. The focus of this book is to guide you in making an app successful. So, can you imagine doing all of these steps for all of your apps? Hopefully, your answer was yes, but once you reach 10-15 apps, this is just unfeasible. Hence, selling the rights to an app is a wise business move to free up some time and make some quick cash. Until about a year ago, only large companies sold app rights, but thanks to some very successful websites that act as brokers, this is now a possibility for all appreneurs. I have sold a few individual apps as well as my entire game guide company.

Depending on your goal, you should proceed accordingly when trying to sell rights. Decide whether you are trying to sell one app, an entire series, or a developer account. If you are trying to sell individual apps, your best option is a site called *www.sellmyapplication.com*. I have had some great results from them. They charge a very reasonable amount to post an ad for your app on their site. One of the key benefits of _www.sellmyapplication.com_ is the size of their community. I have listed quite a few apps with them and usually received inquiries within a day. Furthermore, the seller also gets to interact directly with the buyer, cutting out the middleman and saving you money. This direct buy system works well because no one knows his or her app better than the person selling it. I have not found a better platform for selling an app. They also have a great market for buying preexisting apps and code snippets. I have purchased some awesome code snippets I was able to use in my own apps for a more than reasonable price.

- Selling the rights at the right time

If you make the decision to sell your app or app company, you need make sure it is a decision you will not regret. Usually appreneurs who sell their rights do so when they want to move on to a new series or project and do not have time to maintain their current apps. Finding buyers on your own is almost impossible and more headache than it is worth. When selling my first company, I initially tried to take on the task of finding buyers singlehandedly. It was a daunting and frustrating process that could have been made easier had I known about the team at *www.appbussinessbrokers.com*. I have found this group to be knowledgeable professional brokers. What they do is gather all of the information a potential buyer of your app company will ask and work as a broker. They have a wide client base and can help you sell your apps to investors in a very timely manner. Besides their client base and extensive knowledge of the market, they are also accessible; they even take the time to talk to you on the phone before beginning this process. This is the kind of customer service that makes selling apps less of a hassle.

- Buying pre-established apps

Selling apps is a skill you may have predicted for appreneurs, but as an appreneur, you may also be approached with the unforeseen circumstance of buying apps. Buying apps is generally a business risk, since the majority of apps for sale are trending down and the seller does not know how to reverse the downward spiral. For appreneurs who have the knack for generating sales, what would otherwise be a business risk, may be a business opportunity for you. Before buying, or even considering buying an app, ask yourself these simple questions:

How well established is this app?

If the app has been around for a while, has been ranked fairly consistently, and shows up high in search results, then buying the app may be a great investment. If the app's ranking is way down from its initial release (Remember to use *AppAnnie* to track all of this data), then you are taking a huge risk. Buying this type of app is equivalent to buying a sinking boat while in the water. Sure, you could try and plug the holes and repair it, but it may be sinking so fast that any patch efforts are in vain. The most important factor to consider when buying an app is how well its keywords rank. If an app has established keywords and shows up high in the rankings, then buying the app could be a great move.

How much are they selling the app for?

Price will determine if buying the app is more logical than developing, or having someone develop, something similar. Most studios can give very accurate quotes on what it would cost to build an app similar to something that is already in The App Store. Remember that the only thing you cannot buy when having an app developed is rankings. If the app is ranked well, then do not bother trying to compete and develop your own version.

Do the users like the app?

A cause for concern is if the application is flooded with bad reviews. In this case, you need to be very wary. Last year, some appreneurs developed fake fingerprint scanners, ghost finders, and lie detectors. These apps are just scams, and some poor person downloaded the app thinking it did these things. DO NOT BUY THESE EVER! Apple is cracking down on fraudulent apps and removing them from The App Store; likewise, they are blocking new ones. You will be disappointed when you spend thousands for this app only to have it removed by Apple, or not approved at all. If the seller is willing to scam his users, he will have no remorse in scamming you.

- Selling apps that have never been listed in the app store

In addition to buying and selling preexisting apps, another app opportunity may present itself, "flipping" apps. "Flipping" is a term that originated in the .com era for websites. "Flipping" is where someone builds or buys a website and immediately sells it. Although this has not yet gained popularity in the app world, it is an inevitable eventuality. Already there are a few appreneurs who make similar apps to ones that are popular in The App Store and sell them without ever uploading them to The App Store. This is a huge gamble; you will not know how well the app has done. You won't be able to know if Apple will accept the app, or if it will sell as you expect. Flipped apps are generally less expensive than pre-established apps because of the risk involved. I personally have never bought or flipped an app. It is too much of a risk for me. I have bought and sold plenty of apps but only when I know what to expect. If flipping catches on, then I will adjust my business model, but until then I will stay away from them.

In the next section of the book, I reveal with hesitancy a well-kept secret of mine. Since I decided to hold back nothing in this book, I will reveal how I maximize profit by selling an app's rights at the perfect time. If you are able to successfully follow the trends of your apps and anticipate what will happen well before it does, you can make a considerable profit by selling the rights before your application begins to trend down. One consideration of buyers is how the app is trending. They will usually only be interested in the app if it is trending up or flat. If your app is trending down and you sell it, you will receive fewer offers and less profit. The previous chapters painstakingly described the importance of trend data. It is imperative that you learn how to read this in order to be a successful appreneur. Once you become adept at data analysis, you can make serious money in markets people didn't even know existed. When I foresee an app about to trend down, I put it up for sell at a high price. Ideally, you will have a few very interested buyers very soon because the app is doing well. By doing this, you are maximizing two things, your time and money. If you do not have to worry about re-marketing, re-promoting, and re-advertising an app, then you will have more time to devote in other places. I have found that the best time to sell the rights to apps is in late February, when holiday season sales begin to slow. Typically, your app will trend up during the holiday season; it will likely come down in the spring. If you are able to successfully sell your apps before they trend down, you will make money and fast. This, of course, will not work with every app, but it is a good template to start.

This chapter is probably one of the most complicated in the book. There are many risks associated with buying and selling apps, risks not advisable for the amateur appreneur. I would highly recommend getting some experience under your belt before attempting buying or selling. The app buying and selling world is comparable to the stock market. Do it right and you can make a fortune. Do it wrong and you will lose your fortune... fast.

Appreneurs

Chapter 11

"Keeping piracy to a minimum"

Over the last few years, piracy has become a major problem in The App Store. In 2011, for example, I had twice as many apps pirated as sold. You will hear a lot of naive appreneurs say "Piracy is not a big deal; people that pirate would not have bought your app anyway." This is just flat out wrong. Take the following illustration under consideration. A user pirates the paid version of your app. You are making nothing from them. Following the logic that they would never have paid for it, allows them to download your free, ad backed, version. You will now generate revenue from the user by serving him ads. Users that pirate apps are much less likely to buy them; however, there are plenty of them that will. If you have an application that has server costs, you better make sure you do something to prevent piracy, or these pirates will eat up a ton of your server costs. Believe me it is a dismal feeling when you search your app's name followed by .ipa only to see it all over the internet in every cracked app store. You basically have two options: manually contact each cracked app store and hosting site to deliver them a DMCA (Digital Millennium Copyright Act) to have the app taken down or prevent piracy from ever occurring. My first reaction was to serve DMCA paperwork to each offender. It was the most time consuming and tedious task I have ever initiated. I finally just gave up on trying to prevent piracy on my own. Eventually I was approached by a company called *AntiPi* (*www.antipi.net*), they claimed to be able to prevent piracy. I was skeptical to say the least. I decided it would be worth a try, and I was very happy with the results. This company literally takes down all of your pirated apps from the cracked app stores. Their software inserts within the pirated versions of the apps a legal message followed by only one clickable button "Buy the app in The App Store." This was exactly what I was looking for, a way of converting pirated apps to sales. Obviously, each person that pirated the app is not going to buy it; do not expect that. However, I have noticed about 1:50 do. Although this may sound like a relatively low conversion, these numbers can add up drastically when you consider the thousands of copies being downloaded a day.

Some opinions that are circulating about pirated copies of apps tend to minimize the issue and contend that pirates are actually a form of free advertisement. I disagree wholeheartedly with that notion. First of all, any time your app is pirated, someone has gotten it for free. People that pirate apps are proud of what they do and will often brag about it in your app to other users. I had an app that had a lobby chat room that allowed users to interactively chat. I noticed that once my app became readily available to the cracked app stores, hundreds of people in my chat room were bragging about how they got the app for free. As you can imagine, the users that paid for my app were quite upset with this. The people that were using the pirated version of my app were also using features that required server calls, which cost money. No matter how big or small your app is, piracy will always be a problem and that is why you should do your best to prevent it. I highly recommend *AntiPi* for this. They charge very reasonable rates and take care of all of the grunt work. You also will get a monthly report showing how many copies of your app they kept from the pirates. My first month's report showed over 150,000 total copies prevented from being pirated. Prevention did not result in 150,000 extra sales, but that is still a lot of people who won't be using my app for free and costing me money and headaches.

With jailbreaking becoming easier, I recommend taking action to circumvent piracy. Piracy has the ability to crush industries (Look at what *Napster.com* did to the music industry). No matter how big or small your app is, it is only a matter of time until it gets cracked.

In the last few months Jailbroken devices have been enabled to download in-app purchases for free. Many developers took the route of add in-app purchases in their apps as a way of preventing piracy. This no longer is a viable option. The only in-app purchases that cannot be cracked are server validated, so if you decided to use in-app purchases to circumvent piracy make sure they are server validated.

Appreneurs

Chapter 12

"Evolving with the App Store"

Below is a story from Randal Higgins, founder of *www.touchmint.com*

My path to developing started about a year after college. I graduated with degrees in computer information systems and computer network administration. During college, I took a few programming classes such as Java and Flash, but I was far from good at them. During school I always wanted to develop iPhone apps, but I did not have a Mac and could not justify the cost at the time. About a year after I graduated, I moved to Arizona, sold some electronics and online game items on *Ebay/Craigslist* and finally bought a MacBook pro.

Being a Windows person for most of my life, it was a little hard to figure out the file system and a few other things on the Mac OS. I started learning Objective-C by reading *Programming in Objective-C* by Stephen G. Kochan through Safari Books. The book was a great starter and the Safari Books membership is a must have; they have every programming book you can think of. After *reading Programming in Objective-C*, I started *Head First iPhone* and *iPad Development*. *Head First* is a great hands-on book. It made Xcode very easy to understand.

As I worked through the *Head First* book, I was thinking about an app I wanted to develop. I have always been a huge fan of playing sport, especially the statistics involved. I play quite a bit of softball and had been trying to keep my stats, but all the programs out there lacked. I decided my first app would be a baseball/softball stat-tracking app. Since I had already downloaded all the baseball stat apps on The App Store, I knew what worked and what didn't work. I analyzed user reviews and found what others liked and did not like. I can't stress enough how important it is to know your market and competition. It is not everyone's goal to make money, but if you do plan on making money you better know the market and your competition.

Nowadays I see so many talented people pour so much time into an app that is likely to fail because the app market is flooded with similar apps. Like I said before, I am nowhere close to a good programmer, but I would argue it's more important to know the market.

When I built my first app *Baseball Stats Tracker Touch* it was created as a framework for many other apps. Although it took me about 5-7 months to learn Xcode and build that first app, it was worth it because it was a framework. I have built seven other apps on that framework in just 4 months. All but two apps have reached at least the top 200 in sports. My first app *Baseball Stats Tracker Touch* reached 10th overall in sports and has grossed over 6k in its first 6 months.

About halfway through development, I found a site called *iPhone SDK Forum* that really helped out a ton. To this day, my favorite forum to read is the business and marketing forum. The people there are great, and if you want to learn the ins and outs of the app store that is the place to go.

Just because your app is released does not mean your app is done. A website is a must have which I learned the hard way. I originally built my website *www.touchmint.com* on *Google Sites* which was great because it is free, but my site lacked much customization causing me look unprofessional. I recently moved to *Namecheap* where I have a Wordpress theme; it is just as easy as Google but looks a whole lot better. Ongoing communication is another key to being successful. I make a habit to write back questions and complaints within the hour if possible. It blew my mind that people had never heard back from developers, and they could not believe I was writing them back so quickly. If you really want to keep good reviews, put a support button in your app so people can get support right from your app. I also like to give out promos to my other available apps when someone takes their time to report a bug.

Updating and design are very important factors as well. When your app is targeted towards kids it better look appealing and the icon better be cool. Updates are also great; not only to add new features but also to remind your users they own your app. When they are reminded, they will spread the word about your app.

Overall, I don't think there is a clear one-way path to success but really a combination of many factors. There is a reason why people that know Objective-C and Xcode inside and out have never had a successful app to date. To be successful in The App Store you need have a little of everything. Another important skill is the ability to adjust to app store changes very fast. Apple will change their system, and it's your job as a developer to figure out how to adjust better than the others.

The App Store is evolving every day. It is your job as an appreneur to evolve with it as Randal explained in his testimonial.

Keeping up with The App Store's changes will prepare you to best navigate the app market and make informed appreneur decisions. I have found that the best way to keep updated is a good community. As an active member of the forums at *www.iphonedevsdk.com*, I connect with talented developers and appreneurs. I actually met several of the people whose stories I shared in this book on the forum. Appreneurs who are willing to learn are going to be much more successful than those who are inflexible to change. In this profession, I have found that if you are willing to ask for help, people will be happy to assist you. In particular, the *www.iphonedevsdk.com* forum has provided me with answers to everything app store related. There are thousands of threads available that can answer any type of app related question. My primary use for the forum is to generate other developer's opinions about my ideas. If you are unsure as to why your app isn't meeting your expectations, just simply ask the community. They are fairly blunt, but the criticism is what you may need to help improve your app.

As you near the conclusion of this guide, you should now be equipped to successfully handle every aspect of selling an app. Once you have mastered the information I have given you in this book, you will have no trouble adapting to the ever-changing app store. Evolving with the app store can be as simple as changing your keywords to optimize a new algorithm The App Store may deploy (which changed drastically in 2012) or completely changing your application line to better suit new users. One year, photography apps may be hot, and the next year they may not. You need to be able to transform products as new market trends emerge. Among the many lessons learned from The App Store, it has taught me not to bank on one app producing revenue forever. By examining closely how the top indie developers have made money, it is apparent that they have a wide array of apps, not just one. Banking on one app is a gamble, a risky business move. In the possible event that a competitor makes a better app and you only have that app making money, you're in a very bad position.

Technology is always changing; it is your duty as an appreneur to think of new and innovative ways to include them in your app. One appreneur's story that represents innovation is MobGen's *Alert Tone Creator*. MobGen expertly timed his super simple app that came out with the release of iOS 5. This appreneur did his research and knew that Apple would be allowing custom text tones in iOS 5. Therefore, he integrated this new technology into an easy to use app, an app that became wildly popular. In another example, a few appreneurs made apps that optimized photos for Facebook's new timeline feature. Once again, they knew of a new technology and were able to integrate it at the right time and achieved outstanding results.

Timing is everything when it comes to adding new cutting edge technologies into apps. Generally, if you're not one of the first to do it, then you will not make much money. I like to keep up with current events just for this reason. You don't have to keep up with technology companies to come up with new innovative apps. If you know of something that is hot, or popular, make an app for it. Apple's App Store slogan is "There's an app for that." My favorite part about being an appreneur is the creative freedom I have. Not many jobs allow the creative and personal freedom available to an appreneur. I am able to work doing what I want, when I want.

I am thankful every day I have the opportunity to be an appreneur. You will come to find out how truly awesome the job is. You are on the frontlines of the most cutting edge technology our age has seen. Mobile software is not a fad; it is a new market. Since the invention of the smartphone and tablet, software has been moving from the computers to mobile devices, a transition that will only continue through the years. Are you ready to seize the opportunity?

Chapter 13

"Guest chapter from AppVersal, marketing that works"

In the next subchapter, a company that specializes in mobile app marketing, graciously offers advice on how to differentiate your app from the rest of the market.

- Marketing Your App

This segment of "Marketing your App" has been presented to you by "AppVersal - App Marketing that Just Works". AppVersal markets Apps the right way to reach users and increase sales.

"To me, marketing is all about values. This is a very complicated world. It's a very noisy world, and we are not going to get a chance to get people to remember much about us, no company is. So we have to be really clear on what we want them to know about us."
- Steve Jobs on Brand Value

No matter how good your product is, no matter how beautiful its design appears, no matter how affordable it is, no matter how good it is from the competition, if no one knows about it, it will always fail to reach its potential. Every product needs to be marketed in one way or the other to reach more users and eventually increase sales.

Developing an App is only one half of the battle; marketing is the other. Marketing is not an overnight process. It takes careful planning along with detailed analysis to achieve your desired goals.

There are already over 600,000+ apps in The App Store, and new ones are being added everyday. How do you even think users will discover your app?

You need to reach them; tell them that you have something of value. Here are some tips that would help you market your App the right way.

- App Store optimization

App Store Optimization is the elementary step that you need to undertake in order to successfully market your app. App Store Optimization includes having a proper app description, high ranking keywords, attractive screenshots and better ratings & reviews. The better your app has been optimized for the App Store, the more it ranks for generic search terms and the higher your sales go.

Your App description should be done in such a way that simply sells while capturing the emotions of the user. Your app keywords need to be properly researched, and you should always be testing new keywords that eventually help you rank higher for relevant App Store search terms. Your screenshots should just be ecstatic. Finally, you should have a product that is so enticing that the ratings and reviews automatically take care of themselves.

- Social Media

Social media should be at the core of your marketing plan. You need to be leveraging social media sites like Twitter and Facebook to market your product/service the right way. Use proper tools to gather targeted followers; increase the number of likes on your Facebook page, and you will be soon attracting potential customers towards your offering.

It is a good idea to follow people interested in your niche via Twitter, and try to connect with them to share your product. Two amazing tools that will help you follow as well as unfollow users are *tweepi.com* and *tweetstork.com*.

- Advertising

Advertisements are something that work only if executed properly. With so many platforms available, the number of formats for ads has also gone up. While there is no one particular method that works perfectly, there are many options available at your disposal.

Direct ads allow you to purchase a spot on a particular space on a site for a fixed price for a limited number of days (30 days usually). These ads don't depend on the number of clicks or impressions served. *BuySellAds* works best with respect to this matter.

Google *Adwords* is a very controversial platform. The overall system is confusing with the user interface being complicated. But it works when it does. Choose your specific display networks, choose your keywords, put in some cash, and it could work fantastically for you.

Facebook ads certainly do work. With targeted people available looking for new services to try, Facebook ads are less complicated than Google *Adwords* and works seamlessly.

Retargeting is probably the best available option. With *AdRoll* leading this revolution, we strongly recommend all marketers to look into this option.

- Reviews

The most important element of a successful marketing campaign is to get incredible reviews, both on The App Store as well as via app review websites. Once a user is likely to read a good review about your app, it instantly makes an impression on the customer's mind. It could lead him/her to make a purchase.

Getting reviews on app review sites can be hard. There are just too many app developers like you who are constantly approaching these publishers. You can use a service like reviewRoster.com, which connects developers and publishers to publish reviews of amazing apps. You can also build up an email and send them to app review sites and hope that your app catches their attention. You can also keep submitting to numerous websites constantly; with perseverance, eventually someone will pick up your app.

You need to stay focused and never give up. Getting reviews on app review sites can be a long drawn process, but it is definitely worth the effort.

Better reviews and ratings on The App Store now also have an impact on the way an app ranks for search results. If your app has a better rating than your competition, it is likely to rank higher when somebody searches for something relevant.

- Analytics

Every marketer knows the insane value of analytics. The data is all that matters. Set up an account for *AppFigures*. Keep looking at the reports, countries with most downloads, reviews, and more to successfully pivot your product and constantly keep evolving.

Setup a bit.ly link for your iTunes URL and for just about every promotional tactic; use the bit.ly link to track exactly where users are being driven to your app from.

Sign up with *flurry.com* to get a detailed report on how your App is being used.

Analyze every possible bit of data and only focus on the ones that work.

- Design a Website for the App

Your app needs a home, its very own special place on the web where potential customers can learn all about it, connect with the developers, and follow to stay updated regarding the latest updates. Your app needs a website.

Build just the right website for your app, so users can learn more about your app before making a purchase. Having a website is also better for search engine ranking. Do a decent amount of SEO work on it, and you'll soon notice customers being driven from your site to your iTunes URL and making a purchase.

You can check *AppVersal's* website design process - *http://appversal.com/design.php*

- Videos

A community should be built around your app. Get videos out on YouTube or Vimeo to show users exactly what your app is capable of and what users would be getting out of it. A professional video always helps. There are also thousands of video reviewers on YouTube; contact them and try to get your app reviewed.

- Design

Nothing, believe me, nothing beats good design. Make sure your app icon stands out; your inbuilt graphics should be visually stunning in order to retain users. We won't elaborate much on this, but never ever compromise on the design. As Steve Jobs said, "Design is not the way it looks, it is the way it works".

Use *elance.com* or *99designs.com* to search for a good iPhone UI designer.